National Transformation

Strategic Discipleship from the Church to the Nation in all seven spheres of influence

Biblical Principles and Best Practices for:
Government, Business, Education, Arts/Media, Family, Medicine

Dr. Mark A. Beliles

President, Global Transformation Network and America Transformation Company
Founder, The Providence Foundation and its Biblical Worldview University
Founding Pastor/Apostle, Grace Covenant Church, Charlottesville, Virginia

2018 Copyright by Mark A. Beliles

GLOBAL TRANSFORMATION NETWORK

Global Transformation Network
304 Minor Ridge Rd
Charlottesville, VA 22901
www.NationalTransformation.com

America Transformation Company
www.AmericaTransformationCompany.com

To contact either one:
434-249-4032
Email: NationalTransformation@gmail.com

ENDORSEMENTS BY GLOBAL CHRISTIAN LEADERS

Dr. Mark Beliles has been actively servicing Presidents, Prime Ministers, and other Politicians of many countries by providing mentoring, consulting, and holding seminars, etc. Having seen Pastor Beliles teach in my own church (Hallelujah Community Church, Korea) and having cooperated with him for Transform Korea Connections, I strongly endorse his biblical and transformational perspectives to fellow-ministers and Evangelical cultural leaders around the world.
Revd Dr. Sang-Bok David Kim
Chairman of World Evangelical Alliance

Dr. Mark Beliles brings many years of experience, effectiveness, intregrity and clarity to the challenge of creative cultural change based on the foundational precepts that culture matters and ideas have consequences.
Luis Bush
Transform World Connections

Reformation of the 7 mountains of culture is something that Mark Beliles has been teaching and equipping leaders longer than most. His global Transformation Network across the USA and in 40 other nations has helped leadership teams to develop comprehensive strategic plans that have had outstanding results in governments, businesses and schools. I highly recommend his books and seminars as one of the best resources for pastors and apostolic leaders who have a visión for reformation.
(The Late) Dr. C. Peter Wagner
Wagner Leadership Institute

I have heard Mark Beliles teach and find his message is vital for the church if she is going to take her commission to disciple nations seriously.
Darrow Miller
Co-Founder, Disciple Nations Alliance

We strongly promote and share the life-changing books and teachings of Mark Beliles at our conferences so that Christians may obtain the knowledge of their Christian heritage and experience the transforming effect of it in their lives and their nation.
Joyce and Dave Meyer
Joyce Meyer Ministries

When social action involving Christians is a subject which is disputed and distorted almost daily in the media, I thank God for Mark Beliles and his work in teaching this generation to value and to heed the Christian prinicples which can transform all nations.
(The late) D. James Kennedy
Coral Ridge Presbyterian Church

Mark Beliles had visited and ministered to our churches in Singapore as well as other parts of Asia. He has deep understanding and values of the social-economic and cultural heritage of nations. He brings the biblical perspective of how God had shaped the nations for His purpose and glory. In his messages he stimulate the audience to reflect on the spiritual dimension as we face up the challenge of transformation of our society. His wide knowledge of the historical and cultural roots in the development of nations helps us to play our part to transform our society. I wholeheartedly commend him to you.
Revd Canon Dr. James Wong,
Anglican Church, Singapore

Dr. Mark Belliles is a transformation practitioner with an amazing track record of impacting high level leaders and nations! His scholarly theological and historical work combined with his vast experience in the field, enables him to write on this subject like few can. I highly recommend this and all his books!
Joseph Mattera,
U. S. Coalition of Apostolic Leaders

Your books and training are an excellent resource for us. I believe the Lord has prepared you over the years to be of assistance to our new democratic South Africa.
Kenneth Meshoe
Member of Parliament, South Africa

Table of Contents

Introduction

Section One

1. Introduction to God's Plan for the Nations
2. From Creation to Christ
3. The Christian Era up to c1500
4. 16th Century European Reform
5. United States, the Global South, & Liberty in Modern Times

Section Two

Introduction to Transformation of the key "mountains" or influential areas of culture

6. Church
7. Family
8. Higher Education
9. Arts, Media, Entertainment
10. Business
11. Health, Medicine & Science
12. Government

Section Three

13. The 5 Signs of Transformation of a City or Nation
14. A Practical Agenda for National Transformation

Appendix:
A Self-Assessment for Church Leaders

The Global Transformation Network and additional resources

Biography of Mark Beliles

Introduction

It may surprise the reader but there has never been an example in history where simply a large number of Christians, mega-churches, and so-called "revivals" has completely transformed a nation. An exhaustive study of countries around the world over the two millennia of Christianity confirms that only when such growth also includes an intentional strategy to train and place networked teams of leaders in the most influential institutions of culture does Christianity bring significant change in nations.

So many books are available that do a great job at explaining the importance of prayer, evangelism and planting churches. To bring full transformation and reformation to a nation, we must first transform the beliefs of the people of a nation. This will occur as we preach the gospel, as Jesus commanded, and then teach believers how to live out the truth of the Bible in their everyday life. 2 Chronicles 7:14 reveals to us the importance of repentance and prayer for the transforming of nations. This is obviously where all godly change must begin. No permanent positive change will occur without a heart change first occurring in the citizens of a nation.

But after God changes the hearts of men, what then? When men are changed, their families, businesses, schools, churches, neighborhoods, towns, cities, states, and nations should also change. But this does not always happen today. True revival and awakening will have impact on these areas of culture and their institutions. Second Corinthians 3:17 says that "Where the Spirit of the Lord is, there is liberty." This is true for both men and nations. As the gospel goes into a man's heart, he is changed. He is not perfect, but a new source of authority is established for determining decisions and values for the future. Likewise, as the gospel is infused in the life of nation, the potential for change comes. But for that to really happen, a strategy must be in place.

James Davidson Hunter, sociology professor at the University of Virginia in the United States has confirmed the reality that Christians must have a strategy for discipling the nation in order for it to ever happen. See his recent book called *To Change The World*. Many other books chronicle how the church has discipled nations in the past. Some examples are: *How Christianity Changed the World* by Schmidt, *The Victory of Reason* by Stark, *The Book That Made Your World* by Mangalwadi. And a good book of essays that cites recent examples of discipling nations is *His Kingdom Come* by Stier, Poor and Orvis.

The writer of this book has been traveling in over 50 nations and working with leaders in twice that number since the 1980s and has proven the reality of these observations. This book will seek to build on these and focus on those other tasks that are much too often ignored and de-emphasized by the modern church, but faithfully accomplished by the historic church. We will look at the fundamental best-practices that were followed by the historical church to significantly transform culture. In the Great Commission found at the end of the Gospels Jesus made it clear that evangelism and church had a purpose: to "go . . .and make disciples of all the nations," by "teaching them to observe all that [He] commanded" (Matthew 28:19). To disciple a nation it is best to break it down to its most essential parts. Besides the church, there are at least six other major areas of influence in culture: family, education, health, business, government, and arts/media/entertainment.

Earlier writers and thinkers such as the Dutchman Abraham Kuyper over a century ago spoke of these "domains" or "spheres" of authority and jurisdiction (and Francis Schaeffer, Loren Cunningham, Bill Bright and others have used similar terms and lists in the 1980s). Mark Beliles and Stephen McDowell began teaching about these 7 areas and were the first in recent times to publish books on the reformation of all these 7 areas (with a brief overview of many nations in history where Christianity did bring major change). Since their books emerged around 1990 onward, many people today now teach this way. Popular speakers and books in recent years (such as C. Peter Wagner, Lance Walnau and Johnny Enlow) have called these the seven "mountains" of cultura (or call them "gates" or 'pillars").

Some people make lists that separate arts and media into their own major area and some list science and technology (or make it part of the area of business). Others list education as part of the family area. Others include the poor, disadvantaged and marginalized and leave out the church from the list. [In our view the disadvantaged are not an institution of society, but rather an economic demographic focus, as is children. These are certainly very important for Christians to serve, but does not properly fit in a list of areas or institutions of culture.] There is no single "inspired" list but the seven areas addressed in this book are agreed to by most leaders.

The writer of this book, Dr. Mark Beliles, has consulted with leaders in many nations and worked with various emerging movements that in varying degrees have started to embrace and think how to apply these historic strategies. He teaches things from his study of Scripture and history, but also from his life experience while working personally around the world. One movement is called Transform World with Luis

Bush as its main facilitator. Another is Discipling Nations Alliance with Darrow Miller and Bob Moffat as key facilitators. Others include the International Coalition of Apostolic Leaders with John Kelly as its convening leader, and Advocates International (founded by the late Sam Ericsson), and the Statesman Project and its City Action Councils led by Dennis Peacocke. Global Transformation Network is led by the writer of this book (who also Works closely with the others).

Beliles founded the Providence Foundation and still Works closely with its President Stephen McDowell. Together they co-authored a book entitled *Liberating the Nations* in 1994 that was used in many nations. Now Beliles offers an updated versión of that book, including the main core information but adds insights from his 25 plus years of experience in *Cultural Transformation.* He attempts to provide principles from the Bible that apply to all these areas in the most internationally relevant way possible. The goal is by no means to be exhaustive, but merely introduce in a general way to the citizens of nations a framework for building their societies in accordance with a Biblical view of life. These are drawn not only from Scripture but also from the outstanding example of best-practices that have been applied in history. The ideas here in this book are truly the core practices of the church in history for transforming culture.

It is hoped that this book will help the church see the kingdoms of this world become "the kingdoms of our Lord and of His Christ" (Revelation 11:15).

SECTION ONE

Chapter 1.
Introduction to God's Plan for the Nations

The goal of this book is to equip Christians in the nations around the world with a knowledge of God's hand in their history and through that history rediscover Biblical principles for every key area of national life. The principles we will be learning are from the Creator and therefore valid in every society and in any time in history, not just in one nation or time. God's plan is to bless all nations but today many nations are facing serious problems.

The Bible reveals to us that the world longs for liberation. Romans 8:19, 21 says that "creation eagerly waits for the revealing of the sons of God... because creation itself also will be delivered from the bondage of corruption into the glorious liberty of the children of God" (NKJV). Many statistics show the desperate need for real answers to world problems such as poverty, human trafficking, sexual immorality, abortion, crime, war and refugees, totalitarian governments, and Islamic terrorism.

The Bible says that truth brings freedom (John 8:32). It provides mankind with a theology of liberty that brings real freedom not only to individuals but also nations that are oppressed. From the beginning of time, God created the earth and made man responsible to rule over it. Genesis 1:28 says: "And God blessed them; and God said to them, 'Be fruitful and multiply, and fill the earth and subdue it; and rule over... the earth.'" When man rejected God's Law and lost the ability to not only govern himself, but also to govern society, public tyranny and oppression reigned through sinful men.

Through the death of Jesus Christ the power for both self and civil government was restored to mankind. Though internal liberty was a primary focus of Jesus Christ, it must not be overlooked that His inaugural and farewell sermons both emphasized external civil liberty. In Luke 4:18, Christ's first public message focused on "liberty" for "the poor... the captives... [and] those who are oppressed." It is safe to assume that poverty, slavery, tyranny and injustice were on the Lord's mind when, in His final sermon, He commissioned His followers to "Go therefore and make disciples of all the nations" (Matt. 28:19). Matthew Henry, the great Bible commentator studied by our Founding Fathers, explains that "the principal intention of this commission" is clear. It is to "do your utmost to make the nations Christian nations." This is God's plan for the nations.

The apostle Paul understood this plan very well and sought to communicate it to the Christians of the first century. In 1 Corinthians 6:2 Paul asks a vital question: "Do you not know that the Christians will one day judge and govern the world?" If this is true, Paul says, then they ought to at least be competent to hold public offices such as the local judgeships in Greece. To those Christians in Corinth, as well as in Any nation today, who incorrectly assume that Paul means we should rule **only** in the next age after the second coming of Christ, the next question and answer of the apostle is aimed: "Do you not know that we shall judge angels? How much more the matters of this life?" (vs. 3). Paul then rebukes the Christians for their apathy and irresponsibility that allowed non-Christians to be in control: "If then you have law courts dealing with matters of this life, do you appoint them as judges who are of no account in the church. I say this to your shame" (vs. 4-5).

This shameful situation has become the reality in many nations today. Christians in earlier times used to provide leadership in every area of culture. But today they have largely withdrawn. The battle for God's earth (Psalm 24:1) is being lost today mainly because modern Christians have thought that God does not really care about such things. They fail to see that Christ taught us to focus our prayers, not on heaven, but upon His kingdom coming "on earth as it is in heaven" (Matthew 6:9, 10). The results of such ignorance and neglect of duty has been costly in the last century. Many nations have experienced great revival since 1900, leading to millions of people claiming to be "Christian," yet simultaneously has plummeted into debauchery and corruption at a rate unparalleled in history. In 1900, Africa was about 1% Christian. Today the Christian populace of that continent had grown to about 50%! However, over 75% of Africa lives under totalitarian regimes. Historically, the gospel has liberated nations, but why not in Africa? One primary reason is that Christian missionaries have offered African nations a truncated Gospel message devoid of Biblical answers to anything not strictly of a pietistic or personal nature. This is true now in modern national culture as well. We have many mega-churches in our cities but with only minimal influence.

As a result, these and other nations of the world, have not been presented with a true Biblical theology of liberty and so are being increasingly deceived by Satan's counterfeit. A counterfeit "Liberation Theology" incorrectly identifies the root of public evil as the socio-economic environment, and claims that liberation comes through violent revolution, followed by the people's dependency on a government they can trust. Christ, in contrast, says the root of evil is the heart of man, and therefore, external liberty is possible only when it flows from the internal to the external. Revival therefore must precede Reformation.

Jesus Christ spoke of this "cause and effect" principle in Luke 6:43-45: "For there is no good tree which produces bad fruit; nor, on the other hand, a bad tree which produces good fruit. For each tree is known by its own fruit;... The good man out of the good treasure of his heart brings forth what is good; and the evil man out of the evil treasure of his heart brings forth what is evil."

Every effect has a cause. The fruit is determined by the root. Man's conduct is determined by man's heart. The external is determined by the internal. All external "forms" or structures come from some internal "power." This is the principle of Power and Form. The Christian religion is the essential power needed to create and preserve a form of government that is free and just.

History is Shaped by Man Under the Providence of God

The external affairs of a nation are a reflection of the condition of the hearts of the people. French historian Charles Rollin reflects the view of most eighteenth century writers in stating that God is sovereign over history, but deals with nations dependent upon the heart and action of the people. He wrote: "Nothing gives history a greater superiority to many branches of literature, than to see in a manner imprinted, in almost every page of it, the precious footsteps and shining proofs of this great truth, viz. that God disposes all events as

18

Supreme Lord and Sovereign; that He alone determines the fate of kings and the duration of empires; and that he transfers the government of kingdoms from one nation to another because of the unrighteous dealings and wickedness committed therein."

You cannot understand history without understanding Divine Providence. Providential history is true history. Many modern educators deny the providential view of history and would have us believe that their promotion of one of several "secular" views of history is simply the recounting of plain facts. They fail to tell their students that their own humanistic presuppositions and religious doctrines determine their choice of people, places, principles, and events. They fail to communicate that neutrality is not possible in the teaching of history, for the historian's worldview will dictate his perspective. Even as there are not many interpretations of Scripture (2 Pet. 1:20, 21), neither are there of history—there is really only one correct view; that which is the Author's interpretation and perspective. God is the Author of Scripture and History. History is the autobiography of Him 'who worketh all things after the counsel of His will' (Eph. 1:11) and who is graciously timing all events after the counsel of His Christ, and the Kingdom of God on earth."

The Bible overwhelmingly affirms this truth. Let us examine just a few Scriptures along this line:

Acts 17:24-26—"The God who made the world... gives to all life and breath and all things; and He made... every nation..., having determined their appointed times, and the boundaries of their habitation..."

1 Timothy 6:15-16—"He is the blessed and only Sovereign, the King of Kings and Lord of lords;... To Him be honor and eternal dominion! Amen."

Proverbs 16:9-10—"The mind of man plans his way, but the Lord directs his steps. A divine decision is in the lips of the king."

Job 12:23—"He makes the nations great, then destroys them; He enlarges the nations, then leads them away."

Psalms 22:28—"For the kingdom is the Lord's, and He rules over the nations."

Daniel 2:21—"It is He who changes the times and the epochs; He removes kings and establishes kings."

Daniel 4:17, 26—"The Most High is ruler over the realm of mankind;... Your kingdom will be assured to you after you recognize it is Heaven that rules."

The Providential View of History

The dictionary defines "Providence" as "the care and superintendence which God exercises over His creatures. By 'Divine Providence' is understood 'God Himself.'" Earlier national leaders used many other names for God other than simply "God" or "Jesus." America's first President George Washington used 54 different titles for God in his writings and speeches. Many other previous leaders from various nations in Europe used dozens of titles as well. This reflects the depth of understanding earlier generations had of God and His involvement in human affairs.

Unfortunately the beliefs and worldview of the majority of leaders in earlier times is no longer being taught in schools and popular media. It is absolutely vital that our nation learns of its Providential history once again. As one pastor writes:

"The more thoroughly a nation deals with its history, the more decidedly will it recognize and own an overruling Providence therein, and the more religious a nation it will become; while the more superficially it deals with its history, seeing only secondary causes and human agencies, the more irreligious will it be." A lack of providential education contributes more than any other factor to the rise of secularism in a nation—a separation of history from God as the Author of history.

I'm this past peke

Chapter 2.
From Creation to Christ

Self-government and the Cultural Mandate

Providential history begins thousands of years before many modern nations came into being. To understand a truly Biblical view of the world and of nations we have to start in Genesis. Most Christians today know much about the God-ordained purpose of the family and the church, but very little about the divine institution of government. Genesis teaches about all of it. It shows the main purpose of family is to have children and educate them. But just one walk through a common Christian bookstore shows the lack of material on the subject of government, although the Bible deals with it abundantly.

The history of government also begins in the Garden of Eden. God placed man in the Garden and gave him a cultural mandate to subdue and rule all creatures including himself (Genesis 1:26-28). The test of man's self-government was his ability to resist eating of the forbidden tree without any type of external restraints. He had to internally govern himself to succeed (Genesis 2:16-17). Through Adam's failure to control himself, sin entered into the world and made it difficult for any man thereafter to govern himself. At this time there was no civil government yet to be established. The cultural mandate to Adam did not include the responsibility for ruling over other men. Therefore, when Cain did not control his anger and jealousy, he violently slew his brother in Genesis 4. Who do we see taking responsibility for justice and protection? God Himself. No human authority existed to do it.

Civil Government for Protection

After a period of time, however, the prevalence of sin and lack of self-government led to so much violence that God saw the end result would be all men destroying one another (Genesis 6:5-13). It a genocidal generation where every person was either directly involved in violence or were indirectly complicit by their failure to stop it. Therefore, God decides to intervene and bring a flood as the death penalty for that generation of murderers. He finds one righteous family led by Noah that God brings safely through the flood to a new earth. God re-issues the cultural mandate but now delegates to man the responsibility for governing other men in order to protect human life (Genesis 9:5-7). He does this by telling Noah to henceforth do what God just did – to apply capital punishment for capital crimes, and in general to establish a system of justice for dealing with all crime. This was the beginning of civil government in human history.

Civil government, then, being started by God, is just as much a Divine institution as the Family and the Church. All were established by God with clear purposes and principles of operation revealed in Scripture. Here are some New Testament scriptures defining the purpose of civil government consistent with the story of Genesis 9:

"...governors as sent by him for the punishment of evildoers and the praise of those who do right." (1 Peter 2:13-14)

"...rulers are...a minister of God to you for good. But if you do what is evil, be afraid;... for it is a minister of God, an avenger who brings wrath upon the one who practices evil." (Romans 13:1, 3, 4)

The purpose of government therefore is to protect the life, liberty and property of all individuals, by punishing evildoers and protecting the righteous. When governing rulers refuse to do this, then they themselves are resisting the higher ordinances of God and are illegitimate authorities who should be resisted and replaced by the citizens.

The Origin of Nations

In Genesis 10:4, 20, 31, 32 we find the first reference to "nations" arising from family groups. We also find the rise of pagan monarchy (kingdoms) as the form of civil government in these nations. Centralization of power is a pagan tendency and is also seen in the rise of the first cities such as at Ninevah (Genesis 10:11) and then Babel (Genesis 11:1). Egypt with its "Pharaohs" are mentioned in Genesis 12:10, 15 and nine kings are mentioned in Genesis 14:1, 2. Nimrod, the builder of Babel, was the first dictator, meaning the first government official to corrupt the God-given purpose of government. Let us look at how he did it.

Centralization of Civil Government at Babel

Nowhere in Scripture is civil government said to have responsibility to be provider of jobs or health or education or anything other than protection and justice. But Nimrod began to make the state a "savior" for men by the centralization of its of powers. He promised to "make a name for themselves" by building the tallest buildings and most advanced civilization, but this required their resources and submission to work. The men at Babel began to congregate together rather than spread out and "fill the earth." They wanted to save themselves through the state as their *counterfeit* Messiah. This was the first public expression of statist Humanism where sovereignty was placed in a man or a collection of men rather than God (Genesis 11:1-8).

God saw the danger is the centralization of power and in order to prevent centralized, one-world government, God made diverse languages. This forced a decentralization into language groups that gradually separated and developed distinct ways of thinking and problem-solving that was unique and diverse in each culture. This cultural diversity is an effective deterrent to one-world government to this day. But world history shows that the centralization of power became common in every single pagan nation in antiquity. It is always the pagan way of problem-solving. Empower a man or few at the top to fix things. But God's way is to empower the people.

The Hebrew Republic with Biblical Civil Laws c. 1450 B. C.

As all of the ancient civilizations centralized power, God called Abraham to establish a unique "nation" among the other pagan nations around 2000 B.C. (Genesis 12:2 and 17:6, 10). Abraham built the Hebrew nation based on the Noah model of family-based decentralized government, although he is identified as the "prince" (Genesis 23:6) or leader of Israel who negotiates and battles with Pharoah (Genesis 12:18), kings of of Sodom and Salem (Genesis 14:17, 18), and King of Gerar (Genesis 20:2 and 21:27).

Eventually the Jewish people found themselves as slaves in Egypt and after 400 years God raised up a liberator to lead them out of bondage and into the promised land. At first Moses tried to govern Israel the way he saw in Egypt, a centralized pagan model. But God used Jethro to advise Moses to decentralize power back to the Biblical model. In doing so Moses told the people to "choose" their judges, i.e. governors (Deut 1:9,13,14). This was in effect the first time a system was put in place where the citizens had the power to vote for their civil representatives. Although still maintaining their cultural elders, these elected government officials were called "judges." For the next 400 years the Book of Judges in the bible described their republican governmental history. (It is also worthy of noting that Jethro, who God used to advise Moses to give people the vote, was a man of both Hebrew and Ethiopian ancestry and a priest of God. The counsel of this black clergyman changed the world.)

God established in Israel a decentralized, representative government where every group of 10, 50, 100 and 1,000 families could choose or elect someone to be their judge or ruler. These representatives in the Hebrew Republic met with the unelected "elders" or tribal heads in a civil body known as the "Sanhedrin" which was the 70 "elders" of the Republic. All civil rulers in Israel, even later when they had kings, did not rule unless they obtained the consent of the governed by a covenant with the people.

God also gave Moses a system of law and a constitution for government the nation around 1450 B.C.. THIS "BOOK OF THE COVENANT" AS IT WAS CALLED MEANT A WRITTEN CONSTITUTION. BOOK = WRITTEN. COVENANT = CONSTITUTION. This was different from the rest of the pagan world at the time which had no fixed higher law; law was whatever the monarch said it was. Law was capricious, arbitrary, unequal and random. But the Law in Israel was written on tablets of stone so it was trustworthy and fair for all. All of their civil laws were based upon God's higher fixed law, and not the whim of a dictator nor a mere majority of people. This makes it a republic, not a democracy or monarchy.

It is also important to note that the elders of Israel were civil, not religious offices. Christians in modern churches tend to associate "elder" with a church leader which was different from the Old Testament civil elders. So there was a separation of "church and state." The clergy of the land were the "Priests" and the "Levites" and the "judges" and elders were civil rulers. The priests did not run the government and the judges and elders did not run the religious institutions. So the idea of "theocracy" in Israel can be completely misunderstood if people think it means religious leaders controlling government and imposing and coercing belief through the state. Israel had no such system. Secular people today who fear a modern theocracy hold this distorted view of both biblical and Christian history. People of faith need to be in public life but their method of governing will always be through democratic and constitutional processes and respectful of religious freedom.

From the beginning, God's purpose was not limited to Israel, but he desired that these laws and their blessings might be exported to all nations on earth who had perverted God's plan of civil government into pagan centralized monarchy. By 1120 B.C., however, as Israel backslid from God and their self and family government, there arose very poor and corrupt leadership under their judges (1 Samuel 8:19-20). Pagan monarchy was effective in keeping order but at the high price of oppression, taxation and the loss of much liberty (1 Samuel 8:10-20). Israel, however, conformed to this pagan form of civil government where dominion was turned into domination. From this point forward until the landing of the Pilgrims at Plymouth—almost 3000 years—the entire world would know nothing of full external liberty for the individual man. God raised up "prophets" who were primarily social reformers and statesmen among the people to try and turn Israel back to their God-given constitution and principles, but only had temporary success until the ultimate judgement came and they were exiled or dominated by pagan gentile empires.

Greece and Rome's Pagan Attempts at Civil Liberty c. 500 B.C.

The second major attempt at democratic government in history was in the Greek city-state of the sixth century before Christ. The Athenian lawgiver, Solon, drew up a legal system that would allow the people to make their own laws. Plato and Aristotle emphasized that a just society was one where every man is moved by concern for the common good. These concepts were also embraced by Roman statesmen such as Cicero and Seneca in the second century before Christ. They proposed an impartial system of laws based on Natural Law which, Cicero said, comes from God and originated before "any written law existed or any state had been established."

The Greek and Roman theories were never as democratic as the Hebrew, however, because of their belief in inequality of men. The ideas of democracy and freedom were only extended to certain classes and all others were denied basic rights. Such tyranny eventually produced conflicts in society that led to chaos and disorder. Cicero was murdered and they reverted to complete totalitarianism to restore order. Greek and Roman contributions to democratic ideas were therefore more theoretical than actual, but were helpful to later generations who learned from their mistakes.

The fundamental flaws of their attempts at democracy were rooted in their belief that man was naturally unequal and that only one or a privileged few were competent to govern the rest. The pagan and Christian ideas of man and government are contrasted well by Historian Richard Frothingham. Of this pagan view that dominated the world at this time in history, he wrote: "At that time, social order rested on the assumed natural inequality of men. The individual was regarded as of value only as he formed apart of the political fabric, and was able to contribute to its uses, as though it were the end of his being to aggrandize the State. This was the pagan idea of man. The wisest philosophers of antiquity could not rise above it. Its influence imbued the pagan world;... especially the idea that man was made for the State, the office of which, or of a divine right vested in one, or in a privileged few, was to fashion the thought and control the action of the many."

The Gospel of Jesus Christ Introduces the Christian Idea of Man and Government

With the coming of Jesus Christ and His death on the cross for the sins of the world, man's ability to govern himself internally was restored. The Law of God was no longer an external thing, but now could be written on men's hearts and interpreted not by prophets and judges, but by the Spirit within them.

We have seen how man lost his ability to be self-governed when he disobeyed God. This led to external governmental tyranny. Christ also came to restore to man the potential of being self-governing under God. As mankind begins to be self-governed, it will have an effect on the external government's operating on his life. Jesus came to not only bring internal salvation, but also external political freedom.

After Jesus had risen from the dead and before He ascended into heaven, He gathered His disciples together.

Acts 1:6-8 states "And so when they had come together, they were asking Him saying, 'Lord, is it at this time You are restoring the kingdom to Israel?' He said to them, 'It is not for you to know times or epochs which the Father has fixed by His own authority; but you shall receive power when the Holy Spirit has come upon you; and you shall be My witnesses both in Jerusalem, and in all Judea and Samaria, and even to the remotest part of the earth.'" (Acts 1:6-8).

Of what type of kingdom were Jesus' disciples speaking? They were speaking of an external kingdom. For centuries the Hebrew people had read the prophecies of Scripture declaring a Messiah would come and set up His throne and deliver the people from bondage. While Jesus walked on the earth, many of His followers thought He would set up His reign at any time. They even tried to make Him King. His disciples did not understand how His Kingdom was going to come.

While they had not seen it established during Jesus' ministry on earth, surely now that He had risen from the dead, He would restore the Kingdom. That's why they asked Him this question. Jesus did not deny that an external expression of the Kingdom would come. In fact, He said that times and epochs would follow (which we can look back upon today) that would contribute to the establishment of the Kingdom and the extension of external and internal liberty "to the remotest part of the earth."

But Jesus told them that the "power" for this external establishment of liberty was through the Baptism of the Holy Spirit. He knew the inevitable result of internal liberty would be external liberty. God's pathway to liberty is from the internal to the external. God's desire is for an external expression of His Kingdom on earth. Yet it must first begin in the heart of man, and then it will naturally express itself externally in all aspects of society.

The Bible reveals that "where the Spirit of the Lord is, there is liberty" (2 Corinthians 3:17). When the Spirit of the Lord comes into the heart of a man, that man is liberated. Likewise, when the Spirit of the Lord comes into a nation, that nation is liberated. The degree to which the Spirit of the Lord is infused into a society (through its people, laws, and institutions), is the degree to which that society will experience liberty in every realm (civil, religious, economic, etc.)

Christ came to set us free (Gal. 5:1, 3). Spiritual freedom or liberty ultimately produces political freedom. External political slavery reflects internal spiritual bondage.

Gradual Leavening Principle: Civil Authority Comes Through Service and Work, Not Imposition

But in addition to this internal liberty, Christ also proposed principles for external civil liberty. As the church propagated these principles throughout the pagan world, the Christian idea of man and government became clear. As Frothingham states: "Christianity then appeared with its central doctrine, that man was created in the Divine image, and destined for immortality; pronouncing that, in the eye of God, all men are equal. This asserted for the individual an independent value. It occasioned the great inference, that man is superior to the State, which ought to be fashioned for his use;... that the state ought to exist for man; that justice, protection, and the common good, ought to be the aim of government."

Christianity's method of change is the same for nations as it is for individuals. As Christians, we are gradually transformed as we apply the truth of His word to our lives. Dr. Augustus Neander, a church historian in Germany, reveals in his 1871 book, *General History of the Christian Religion,* how Christianity has historically brought about change in various nations of the world. Neander writes:

"Again, Christianity, from its nature, must pronounce sentence of condemnation against all ungodliness, but at the same time appropriate to itself all purely human relations and arrangements, consecrating and ennobling, instead of annihilating them... That religion which aimed nowhere to produce violent and convulsive changes from without, but led to reforms by beginning in the first place within,—whose peculiar character it was to operate positively rather than negatively, -to displace and destroy no faster than it substituted something better..."

Christian reforms within a nation do not begin with external or violent means (quite a contrast to Marxist/Communist "reforms" we see today), but they begin within.

In dealing with unbiblical situations in the nations today, we must remember that reform begins within, and as we remove the bad we must simultaneously substitute something. A government-controlled and funded welfare system is unbiblical, yet the solution is not to pass a law that immediately eliminates civil government support of the needy. Individuals and churches must begin to fulfill their God-given responsibility in this area (substitute the good) as we remove the role of our civil government.

Neander goes on to say: "Yet Christianity nowhere began with outward revolutions and changes, which, in all cases where they have not been prepared from within, and are not based upon conviction, fail of their salutary ends. The new creation to which Christianity gave birth, was in all respects an inward one, from which the outward effects gradually and therefore more surely and healthfully, unfolded themselves to their full extent."

External liberty, then, must come gradually, not immediately. It was this mindset of immediate civil change that Christ sought to change in His parable found in Luke 19:11-17. The "nobleman" in the parable, who is a type of Christ, emphasizes to his servants that their responsibility is to "occupy" or "do business" with their earthly finances, time and talents until He returned. The reward for the faithful was that they would be given "authority over cities." Their labor naturally produced a profit, but the reward here was something completely different and unexpected: civil authority.

In other words, Jesus was giving a clue to Christians as to how to gain control of civil government. It is not to be imposing it upon people, but by consistent hard work and service to meet the needs of society around us. It comes about through democratic process, not by usurpation of power. Be the best at your business and you will be called upon to solve problems and lead in your community.

Christ's Teachings on Politics and Government

Knowing that internal liberty would move outward, Jesus provided some principles and guidelines on civil government. These include:

1. Government exists to serve the common good of every individual

When we read the familiar passage of Matthew 20:25-28 in context, we receive a broader view of what Jesus meant. "But Jesus called them to Himself, and said, 'You know that the rulers of the Gentiles lord it over them, and their great men exercise authority over them. It is not so among you, but whoever wishes to become great [i.e. a governor] among you shall be your servant..."

Jesus is making reference to civil authorities, and is declaring that they are to be public servants. Therefore, the purpose of civil government is to serve people. This was a radical, new idea, and it contrasted greatly with the pagan idea of rulers dominating the people, an idea which existed throughout the entire world at this time.

As we will see, this idea gradually leavened many nations of the world, especially the United States. Today we call our civil leaders "public servants." Many governments today use the term "minister" or "prime minister" because of this teaching of Christ. That the civil government is the servant of man is a Christian idea.

2. Civil Government must be limited and separate from the Church's Jurisdiction

While God cannot be separated from government, the Bible does speak of limits of jurisdiction of the state and church. Jesus taught that we are to render "to Caesar [the state] the things that are Caesar's, and to God the things that are God's." (Matt. 22:17-21).

One thing that belongs to the state and not the church is the use of the sword to protect the citizenry (Rom. 13:1-4). Some things that belong to God and not the state include our worship of God, our children, and our own consciences and lives. In these matters, the state has no authority and should not interfere.

Three views of this "church/state" issue exist today. They can be summed up by the following:

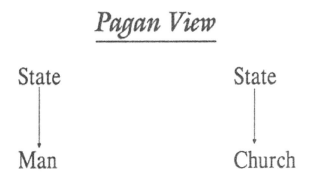

Here the state is sovereign over man and the church and dictates in civil and religious matters. Communism operates according to this idea.

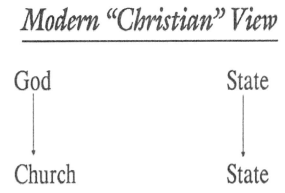

Many Christians today acknowledge that God is sovereign over the Church, but do not believe He has anything to do with the state. God is separated by an impregnable wall from government.

Biblical View

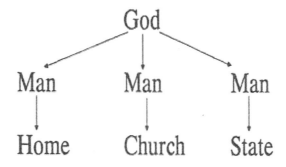

God is sovereign over man, out of which flows the state, the church and the home. Each has a separate jurisdiction, and must be kept separate.

God is sovereign over man, out of which flows the government of the state and the church and the home. Each has a separate jurisdiction, and must be kept separate.

3. Protest or Legal Action against Unjust government

There may come a time when we must resist unlawful authority. If so, we must be prepared to suffer the consequences, but we must also recognize that there are steps we should take in our resistance. A tyrant is one who exercises unlawful authority. Our first means of recourse should be to protest and/or to take all legal action possible. Jesus protested when He remained silent before Pilate and refused to cooperate (Mt. 27:14) and when He publicly censured Herod for his death threats (Luke 13:31-32).

He also instructed His disciples to publicly protest if city officials denied them their inalienable right to religious speech. He told them to go out into the streets and say, "Even the dust of your city which clings to our feet, we wipe off in protest against you" (Luke 10:11). "Wiping off the dust" is equivalent to boycotting. The Apostles followed these instructions and protested and took legal action. When Paul and Barnabas were driven out of Antioch by the city officials, "they shook off the dust of their feet in protest against them" (Acts 13:51) as Jesus had instructed them.

In Acts 16 we read how Paul and Silas were unlawfully thrown into jail. When the chief magistrates tried to cover this up, Paul, recognizing his civil liberties were a sacred cause, demanded restitution to be made. "Paul said to them, 'They have beaten us in public without trial, men who are Romans, and have thrown us into prison; and now are they sending us away secretly? No indeed! But let them come themselves and bring us out.'" (Acts 16:37). The chief magistrates did come and bring them out themselves. When Christians have practiced saying "no!" against tyranny they have changed history.

The reason Paul appealed to Caesar in Acts 24-26 was because his civil rights had been violated. He was being a good steward of the civil liberties God gave to him. The whole course of Paul's life was changed due to his exerting his rights as a citizen. He saw this action as part of the Great Commission.

Protesting unlawful action is a Christian idea. "Protestants" originally received this title, not because they had great revival meetings and church growth, but due to their protesting against authorities (civil and ecclesiastical). Their protest is what made the Reformation effective to transform Europe. Later people such as Martin Luther King, Jr. effectively reformed America by teaching African-Americans to do this. And even when non-Christians apply Biblical methods for resisting tyranny they find some measure of success. An example is Gandhi in India.

The free nations of the world generally have more means of legal recourse and of protesting ungodly action than do others. Examples of protesting include picketing abortion chambers, boycotting stores that sell pornography, and removing our children from public schools that deny God. We who live in free nations not only have the right to do this but are obligated to God to do so to keep our consciences clean. But is far more dangerous when a Christian protests in a tyrannical country.

4. Separation or Flight

If all avenues of protest or legal action are expended to right unlawful acts of civil authorities, than flight, if possible, is the next appropriate measure to take. Jesus told His disciples that "whenever they persecute you in this city, flee to the next" (Mt. 10:23). He also warned them to flee the destruction that was to come upon Jerusalem (Mt. 24:15-18). The early church also took flight as persecution rose against them (Acts 8:1-4). Sometimes flight to other places will more surely allow us to obey god and fulfill His will.

Many people who came to settle in the United States of America were fleeing civil and religious tyranny. After exhausting all means of protest and legal action, they saw that flight was the best means of accomplishing God's purpose. This principle is the basis of the Constitutional right of emigration.

5. Authorized Force in self-defense

As a last recourse in resisting tyranny, force is a legitimate biblical means. The Old Testament contains many examples of the Children of Israel using force to defend themselves. We will examine in a later lesson how a defensive war in a just cause is sinless, but for now we want to show that Jesus also considered force legitimate at certain times in resisting tyranny.

At the conclusion of the Last Supper, Jesus finished His instructions he began with the Seventy by instructing His disciples to prepare themselves militarily, "'Let him who has no sword sell his robe and buy one.' And they said, 'Lord, look, here are two swords.' And He said to them, 'It is enough.'" (Luke 22:36, 38), implying the legitimacy of using force at certain times.

John Jay, the first Supreme Court Justice of the United States, commented on this in a letter written in 1818:

"Although just war is not forbidden by the gospel in express terms, yet you think an implied prohibition of all war, without exception, is deducible from the answer of our Lord to Pilate, viz: 'If my kingdom were of this world, then would my servants fight, etc.' [Yet] At the conclusion of the Last Supper, our Lord said to his disciples: 'He that hath no sword, let him now sell his garment and buy one.' They answered: 'Lord, here are two swords.' He replied: 'It is enough.' It is not to be presumed that our Lord would have ordered swords to be provided, but for some purpose for which a sword was requisite. When the officers and their band arrived, with swords and with staves, to take Jesus, they who were about him saw what would follow. 'They said unto him: Lord, shall we smite with the sword?'" (Luke 22:49). It does not appear that any of the eleven disciples were with him, except one, made the least attempt to defend him. But, Peter, probably inferring from the other swords, that they were now to be used, proceeded to 'smite a servant of the high-priest, and cut off his right ear' (vs. 50). "Jesus (perhaps, among other reasons, to abate inducements to prosecute Peter for that violent attack) healed the ear. He ordered Peter to put his sword into its sheath, and gave two reasons for it. The first related to himself, and amounted to this, that he would make no opposition, saying: 'The cup which my Father hath given me, shall I not drink?' The second related to Peter, viz., they who take the sword, shall perish by the sword; doubtless meaning that they who take and use a sword, as Peter had just done, without lawful authority, and against lawful authority, incur the penalty and risk of perishing by the sword. This meaning seems to be attached to those words by the occasion and circumstances which prompted them. If understood in their unlimited latitude, they would contradict the experience and testimony of all ages, it being manifest that many military men die peaceably in their beds."

As Jay noted, Christ's mission precluded the use of force in this particular instance, nonetheless, Jesus taught the legitimacy of using the legal defensive sword to restrain the illegal sword of an aggressor (Mt. 26:52). The authority and responsibility of using the sword to punish evil or protect the righteous (either from within a nation or from foreign aggression) resides with the civil government (Rom. 13:1-4). That is why anytime we reach the step where force is necessary in resisting tyranny, we must go through legitimate governing officials who will authorize our actions. A lower representative must be convinced to ignore a higher decree in obedience to

God's higher law. Those who disobey an ungodly law or ruler must be prepared to pay the price for such an action.

Go and Disciple The Nations

Having taught all these principles Jesus gathered his disciples just prior to his ascension into heaven in order to give them their mission. He said that they were to go and "make disciples of all the nations" (Mt 28:19-20). By putting the word "nations" there, Jesus' Great Commission to His followers was much more than merely winning souls for heaven. It included a responsibility to transform the societies where we live on earth. The early Apostles understood this very well and the history of early Christianity shows their comprehensive kind of ministry in every sphere of life – family, business, schools, arts and media, medicine, government – not just in growing churches.

Chapter 3.
The Christian Era up to c1500

The Chain of Liberty Moves Westward to Europe

The Primitive Churches in the Roman Empire 33-312

As the early Church applied the political principles that Jesus taught, they not only affected multitudes of lives, but also turned the entire known world upside down. Paganism was being overthrown throughout Europe as Christianity rapidly spread. By 500 A.D. about 25 % of the world had become Christian and over 40% had been evangelized.

In the previous chapter we have already documented the frequent instances in the New Testament where the apostles resisted tyranny by various forms of civil protest and legal action (Acts 13, 16, 24, 25, 26). The first chapter of this book mentioned how the apostle Paul rebuked the Christians in Greece for their apathy and irresponsibility in regards to politics that allowed non-Christians to be in control (1 Corinthians 6:2-5). He urged them to seek public office such as in the local court system of Corinth. When the Christians found it difficult to make inroads in the Roman legal system, they began to form their own alternative courts, which were binding only upon those who voluntarily accepted the outcome by covenant agreement. Over time, the pagans began to reject the arbitrary Roman system and seek for real justice through the Christian courts. By the time of Constantine around 300 A.D., half of the empire's population had been converted to Christianity and consequently were involved in the "Christian" court system. Thus when Constantine made Christianity the official established religion of the empire, the Christian judges were also given legal status and therefore required to wear the official dark robe or gown worn by all civil magistrates. The modern practice of mainline denominational clergymen wearing "pulpit gowns" traces its origins to this act, because most of these "Christian judges" were clergymen. The "pulpit gown" therefore is a testimony and memorial of the primitive churches being involved in politics.

Paul's exhortation to these Christians in Corinth was so strong that one of Paul's own staff—a man named **Erastus**—eventually switched from being a gospel minister to become a civil "minister" (Romans 13:4, 6—"Rulers are servants of God... a minister of God to you for good.."). Erastus had been a full-time apostolic assistant to Paul, just like Timothy, until he was sent by Paul over to Greece (Acts 19:22). While ministering to the churches there, Erastus began to feel God's calling into political office. Paul tells us what happened to him when, in the close of his letter to the Romans (written from Corinth), Paul says: "Erastus, the city treasurer greets you" (Romans 16:23). Archaeology has uncovered in Corinth a first-century tablet that reads: "Erastus, the Commissioner of Public Works, laid this pavement at his own expense." This is believed to be the Erastus of the Bible.

What an exciting illustration of obedience to Christ's command to his disciples to be public servants once they gain positions in government! Here Erastus does something unprecedented in pagan Roman government—he personally pays for the project instead of raising taxes—and is honored with a special tablet. Here we have an example in the New Testament of Christians, not just protesting evil government, but taking the initiative to provide good government by seeking civil office—and its sanctioned by the greatest apostle of all!

Besides all this, the primitive churches provided a model of self-government with union among their congregations. Although church government on the local level was predominantly self-governing, nonetheless, there were certain limited powers in the hands of the apostles and elders of the churches at large who met in council at Jerusalem (Acts 15:2, 4, 6 and 16:4) and approved special ministries such as a poor fund which was administered out of Jerusalem (Galatians 2:1, 2, 9 and 2 Corinthians 8:19, 23). The relationship between the mother church in Jerusalem and all the other new churches was the first example of federalism, or dual governments working both at once in defined spheres of jurisdiction (local and national).

As the centuries went on, the church gradually lost its virtue and Biblical knowledge and thus embraced a pagan philosophy of government and education. This caused them to think that only they could understand God's Word and, therefore, must tell the people what God required of them, instead of allowing every person to be self-governing and learn for themselves.

Instead of sowing the truth in the hearts of the people and allowing the inevitable fruit to grow, the clergy simply tried to externally dictate to the people what they thought God commanded (and what they thought was often quite contrary to the Bible). The first pagan king to be converted was the king of Armenia in 295 A.D. He declared his nation to be "Christian" although it was not genuine. It was still a pagan form of monarchical government.

Constantine also attempted to accomplish God's will with pagan methods. After Constantine was converted (about

312 A.D.) he desired to make his empire Christian. Yet not understanding God's method of gradualism, he superficially united the Church and State and set up a national church declaring all citizens in his empire must be Christians. His attempt at accomplishing that which was good, hindered the work of God for centuries to follow in an era which became known as the "Dark Ages," which followed the fall of the Roman Empire in 410 A.D.

Patrick, Alfred and the Law of Moses in Britain

Christianity was introduced in Britain in the first century, possibly by Joseph of Arimathea. As the Celts were converted they established decentralized churches, unlike those that developed in the Roman and Byzantine Empires. By A.D. 150 the Pastors of the Celtic Churches preached in the common language from interlinear Bible translations called glosses.

The greatest of the pastors was Patrick who left England and went to evangelize Ireland. King Loeghaire was converted and made Patrick his counselor (termed "Annchara") and thus Biblical Law began to be introduced into the civil realm. In 432 Patrick wrote liber Ex Lege Moisi (Book of the Law of Moses) which was applied by local chieftains or kings throughout Ireland (as yet not a united political arrangement, only a Biblical/religious unity). It emphasized the rule of law and local self government.

The Anglo-Saxons first came to Britain around 428 A.D. when two brothers, Hengist and Horsa, were invited to bring their relatives and help the king of Kent fight off his enemies. They stayed in Britain, and after some time eventually took the island over and named it Anglo-land, or Engel-land (today England).

Initially the Anglo-Saxons turned on the Celts, killing many of them. One time they killed 1200 Celtic Pastors in prayer. However, while the Saxons conquered the Celts militarily, the Celts conquered the Saxons spiritually. The Saxons were thus converted to Celtic Christianity. Catholicism did not come to Britain until 597. After its introduction the church in Britain, due to the Celtic influence, still emphasized the Bible above Papal authority.

Around 565 a follower of Patrick, named Columba, left his Ireland and evangelized the king of the Picts (who lived in what is today Scotland). Columba also translated liber in the Scottish language.

The first king who was revered enough to unite all of England into one nation was known as **Alfred the Great**, who ruled from 871 to 899. After defeating the Vikings and uniting England, Alfred instituted Christian reforms in many areas including establishing a government that served the people. Alfred was taught how to read by a Celtic Christian scholar known as Asser, and studied Patrick's liber and thus established the Ten Commandments as the basis of law and adopted many other patterns of government from the Hebrew Republic. The nation organized themselves into units of tens, fifties, hundreds and thousands and had an elected assembly known as the "Witen." These representatives were called respectively: a tithingman (over ten families), a vilman (over 50), a hundredman, and an earl. The earl's territory which he oversaw was called a "shire," and his assistant called the "shire-reef," where we get our word "Sheriff" today. The Witen also had an unelected House made up of the nobleman, but the king was elected; he was not a hereditary king. Their laws were established by their consent. Alfred's uniform code of Laws was the origin of common law, trial by jury, and habeas corpus. Alfred's code was derived from Mosaic law and Jesus' golden rule.

Reaching its height in the late 800's under the Christian King Alfred, Anglo-Saxon law was eroding at the time of the Norman Conquest over two centuries later in 1066. The Normans, under William the Conqueror, established a royal dynasty—a system which destroyed the rights of the people yet increased efficiency by centralization of common law under Henry II.

Meanwhile, in 1016, Iceland became a Christian nation by genuine democratic process. The "Holy Roman Empire," founded by Otto I, King of Germany, in 962 A.D., launched a series of 8 crusades to "liberate" the Holy Land from the Muslims (1095 -1272). At the apex of the Medieval Papacy under Pope Innocent III, a significant step toward liberty occurred in England.

Magna Charta 1215

In England, the Norman system of government removed the rights of the people. Consequently, the kings abused the people, barons as well as commoners.

Things worsened to the point under King John that the English barons drew up a contract that addressed the abuses and guaranteed the barons certain rights and privileges as contained in Biblical law. King John, needing the help of the barons to raise money, reluctantly signed the Magna Charta in 1215. It is interesting to note (but not surprising) that a clergyman, Stephen Langton, is likely the chief architect of the document. The Pope said it was illegal but the English Catholic Church, having Celtic origins, ignored the Pope and preserved the document and expounded it (rather than the government).

The Magna Charta embodied the principle that both sovereign and people are beneath the law and subject to it. Later, both Englishmen and American colonists cited the Magna Charta as a source of their freedom.

It is also notable that around 1200, a Catholic monk named Dominque in England instituted the first example of representative government on a national level in England in his Order of Monks. This was in great contrast to most of Catholicism. Around 1300 Parliament was created reflecting the representative principle.

In 1231 the Pope initiated the first phase of the Inquisition to identify and punish "heretics."

John Wycliffe in England 1382

The time period from approximately 500 -1500 A.D. was called the Dark Ages because mankind generally was stagnant and saw little or no advancement in civil liberty, scientific discoveries, technology, and almost every other area. This lack of advancement was primarily a result of the light of the Word of God being "hidden" from the common people. The Word of God was completed by the apostles in the first century and canonized in the following few centuries; yet as the church "backslid" from God, His Word was further removed from the people. Nevertheless, "the textbook of Liberty" was providentially being preserved by scribes and monks who painstakingly spent their entire lives hand-copying the Bible.

The lack of access to the truth of the Bible kept the common people ignorant during the Dark Ages. Around 1348, the bubonic Plague killed one third of the population of Europe. Shortly after this a Catholic clergyman named John Wycliffe, who did have access to the truth, began to see that "Scripture must become the common property of all" that there might be "a government of the people, by the people, and for the people." To accomplish this goal, he translated the whole Bible from Latin into English. This was completed around 1382, one hundred fifty years before the Reformation occurred.

He not only translated the Bible, but set out to implant the truth of the Scriptures in the hearts of all men. This was accomplished by distributing Bibles, books of the Bible, and tracts throughout all England.

His followers, called "Lollards" (a derogatory term meaning "idle babblers"), would travel to towns and villages passing out Bibles and tracts and preaching and teaching on street corners, in chapels, gardens, assembly halls, and everywhere else they had an opportunity. As most people were uneducated, the Lollards taught many how to read, including many nobles.

In the words of German Professor G. V. Lechler, the Lollards "were, above all, characterized by a striving after holiness, a zeal for the spread of scriptural truth, for the uprooting of prevalent error, and for Church reform. Even the common people among them were men who believed; and they communicated, as by a sacred contagion, their convictions to those around them. Thus they became mighty."

The translation of the Bible in the hands of the Lollards became such a power, that at the close of the century, "according to the testimony of opponents, at least half the population had ranged themselves on the side of the Lollards."

As prevalent error in the church began to be add... church leaders showed their appreciation by try... eradicate this *heretical* movement. Over the decades, ... were able to stomp out most of the effects of Wycliffe's wor... and drive his followers underground, but the seeds of truth had been planted, that would later spring forth and produce a Reformation that no man could stop.

In 1425, hoping to remove all the traces of Wycliffe's *treachery,* the church ordered his bones exhumed and burned along with some 200 books he had written. His ashes were then cast into the little river Swift, "the little river conveyed Wycliffe's remains into the Avon, the Avon into the Severn, the Severn into the narrow seas, they to the main ocean. And thus the ashes of Wycliffe are the emblem of his doctrine, which now is dispersed all the world over."

With John Wycliffe, the "Morning Star of the Reformation", the first rays of the light of God's Word began to shine forth in the darkness. This coincided with the beginning of the "Renaissance" (1340 to 1540) or revival of Greek and Roman art and learning.

The Printing Press in Germany 1455

An event occurred in the 15th century that assured that the light of the truth would never be put out by any civil or ecclesiastical government. That event was the invention of the printing press by John Guttenberg around the year 1455.

The first book printed by Guttenberg was the Bible. Before this time, the only means of recording was by hand. It would take scribes over a year to hand copy one Bible. It's no wonder Bibles were scarce and expensive.

ry as the Reformation broke forth, the use
ess was instrumental in spreading the
'. Within 10 years of the invention of the
ber of books increased from 50,000 to 10
in wrote:

...through the energizing influence of the printing press, emperors, kings, and despots have seen their power gradually waning, and the people becoming their masters."

Christopher Columbus in Spain 1492

The Catholic monarchs of Spain, however, came under the influence of a man whose name meant "The Christbearer" who believed that it would be possible to reach the east by sailing west. In 1492, Christopher Columbus opened up the New World to civilization.

We all know of this event, but do we know what motivated Columbus to embark on such an arduous and dangerous journey? The following excerpts from his diary will tell us:

"It was the Lord who put it into my mind—I could feel His hand upon me—the fact that it would be possible to sail from here to the Indies...

"All who heard of my project rejected it with laughter, ridiculing me... There is no question that the inspiration was from the Holy Spirit, because He comforted me with rays of marvelous illumination from the Holy Scriptures... For the execution of the journey to the Indies, I did not make use of intelligence, mathematics, or maps. It is simply the fulfillment of what Isaiah had prophesied...

"No one should fear to undertake a task in the name of our Savior, if it is just and if the intention is purely for His

Service... The fact that the Gospel must still be preached to so many lands in such a short time—this is what convinces me."

While Columbus discovered the New World, God did not allow the country from which he sailed to colonize the territory which originally comprised the United States. Colonization occurred in much of South and Central America and in 1493 the Pope gave Africa, Asia, and Brazil to Portugal and the rest of Latin America to Spain. In 1497, John Cabot, landing near the St. Lawrence River, laid claim to America for England. At this time, England, as all of Europe, lived under civil and religious tyranny, yet as we have already seen, God would be at work in the sixteenth century to assure that this was changed.

Columbus and other Spanish and Portuguese explorers carried with them the seeds of religious tyranny but American historian Daniel Dorchester writes: "While thirst for gold, lust of power, and love of daring adventure served the Providential purpose of opening the New World to papal Europe, and Roman Catholic colonies were successfully planted in some portions, the territory originally comprised within the United States was mysteriously guarded and reserved for another—a prepared people."

The intervening century was in many respects the most important period of the world; certainly the most important in modern times. More marked and decided changes, affecting science, religion, and liberty, occurred in that period than had occurred in centuries before; and all these changes were just such as to determine the Christian character of the United States differently than lands to its south. What was it that prepared them to settle their colonies differently from those in Latin America? It was a movement that began in Germany by a man named Martin Luther.

Chapter 4.
16th Century European Reform

Martin Lather in Germany 1482-1546

The Roman Catholic Church over many centuries always had some significant thinkers that affirmed individual human rights and liberty. And there were many sincere priests in the church that worshipped the true and living God of the Bible. But it cannot be denied that overall in Europe there was much corruption that needed to be addressed.

Martin Luther was God's instrument to awaken the conscience of man. His act of nailing his 95 theses on the door of the church where he served as a priest at Wittenberg in 1517 is often referred to as a beginning point of the Protestant Reformation. Yet seeds of the Reformation had been planted many years before. About 100 years before, Jan Hus was burned at the stake for stressing Scripture authority instead of corrupt papal authority. He was directly influenced by Wycliffe's works. Hus influenced Luther by his example.

Luther's defense at the Diet of Worms in 1521 reveals that which characterized his life:

'"I am," he pleaded, 'but a mere man, and not God; I shall therefore defend myself as Christ did,' who said, 'If I have spoken evil, bear witness of the evil'... For this reason, by the mercy of God I conjure you, most serene Emperor, and you, most illustrious electors and princes, and all men of every degree, to prove from the writings of the prophets and apostles that I have erred. As soon as I am convinced of this, I will retract every error, and will be the first to lay hold of my books, and throw them into the fire... I cannot submit my faith either to the Pope or to the councils, because it is clear as the day that they have frequently erred and contradicted each other. Unless, therefore, I am convinced by the testimony of Scripture, or by clear reasoning, unless I am persuaded by means of the passages I have quoted, and unless my conscience is thus bound by the Word of God, I cannot and will not retract; for it is unsafe and injurious to act against one's own conscience. Here I stand, I can do no other: may God help me! Amen.'"[11]

His life, and those of the reformers, can be summed up in the Latin phrase, *sola scriptura,* "Scripture alone." He translated the first German Bible in 1534. That was to be the basis of the reformers' thoughts and actions, rather than the decree of pope or king. It was Luther who brought forth out of darkness the great truth that we are justified by faith.

In 1540 Denmark, Norway, and Sweden became Lutheran nations. The movement began to spread widely.

John Calvin and Switzerland 1509-1564

In 1534, when the French Protestant, John Calvin was 25, after having met with his cousin Robert Olivetan and Lefevre (the Bible translators), he left the Roman church in Noyon, France and was put in prison briefly. After his release, he lived in Paris for awhile in disguise and worshipped at secret meeting places in homes and in the woods by using passwords. But, later that year, he fled to Germany and then to Geneva, situated next to Lake Leman. This city had officially voted to be Protestant as a result of seeds planted by Ulrich Zwingli who was killed in battle in 1531 while serving as chaplain in the Swiss army. In 1536, he wrote his famous *Institutes of Christian Religion.* In 1538, the Council of Geneva ordered Calvin to do something that he felt conscience bound to disobey. Then he was banished from Geneva and went to Strasbourg and pastored a French refugee congregation for three years where he also married a French refugee named Idelette. In 1541, Calvin was invited back to Geneva by the Council, and he wrote his *Ecclesiastical Ordinances,* which included policies for jails, education, and the physical health and safety of citizens, such as sanitation requirements.

The writings of John Calvin have probably had more impact upon the modern world than any other book, except the Bible. "No writing of the Reformation era was more feared by Roman Catholics, more zealously fought against and more hostilely pursued, than Calvin's Institutes."[12]

In his history of the Reformation, an author from Switzerland by the name of D'Aubigne writes:

"The renovation of the individual, of the church, and of the human race, is his theme...

"The reformation of the sixteenth century restored to the human race what the middle ages had stolen from them; it delivered them from the traditions, laws, and despotism of the papacy; it put an end to the minority and tutelage in which Rome claimed to keep mankind forever; and by calling upon man to establish his faith not on the words of a priest, but on the infallible Word of God, and by announcing to every one free access to the Father through the new and saving way—Christ Jesus, it proclaimed and brought about the hour of Christian manhood.

"An explanation is, however, necessary. There are philosophers in our days who regard Christ as simply the apostle of political liberty. These men should learn that, if they desire liberty outwardly, they must first possess it inwardly...

"There are, no doubt, many countries, especially among those which the sun of Christianity has not yet illumined, that are without civil liberty, and that groan under the arbitrary rule of powerful masters. But, in order to become free outwardly, man must first succeed in being free inwardly...

"The liberty which the Truth brings is not for individuals only: it affects the whole of society. Calvin's work of renovation, in particular, which was doubtless first of all an internal work, was afterwards destined to exercise a great influence over nations.[13]

Calvin worked hard to make Geneva a model of Biblical government. He established the first Protestant university in history known as the Geneva Academy whose rector was Theodore Beza. Geneva became a centre of reform for not only Huguenot but also Protestant refugees from all over Europe. Puritan leaders of England, as well as John Knox of Scotland, studied under Calvin at Geneva.

The Huguenots: The Protestants in France 1523-1598

In 1523, just one year after Luther's New Testament translation into the German language and two years prior to Tyndale's English translation, Jacques Lefevre d'Etaples published the New Testament in French. The whole Bible was available in 1530 known as the *Antwerp Bible.* Another translation by Pierre Robert Olivetan was published in 1535. (It was revived in 1557 and became known as the Geneva Bible.)

Olivetan's cousin, John Calvin, fled persecution in France and settled in Geneva where he established a training center for many French Protestants. These Protestants became known as "Huguenots" which is a term from a German word meaning "confederates". Despite severe oppression, the Huguenots grew until in 1553 five were publicly burned at the stake. This event, instead of quenching the movement, fueled it so that four years later one third of all Frenchmen were Protestants! (300,000).

Two years later in Paris, a national synod convened and wrote the *Confession of Faith of the Reformed Churches* and the Pope responded by making the reading of the Bible illegal. Three years after this, in 1562, churches grew from 300 to 2000 throughout the land, and because of severe violations of their religious freedom they formed a political alliance to protect it. This plunged the nation into civil war between Protestant and Catholic powers which did not end until the *Edict of Toleration of 1598,* which guaranteed religious and political freedom in certain partitioned areas of the country.

In 1572, 30,000 Protestants were massacred while worshipping on St. Bartholomew's Day. The Huguenots became convinced of the necessity of using force in self-defense and articulated their Biblical reasoning of this in their *Vindicae Contra Tyrannos (A Defense of*

Liberty Against Tyrants) in 1579. This document, drafted by Philippe DuPlessis Mornay, drawing from reasoning found in Calvin's writings, became a precedent for the American Colonists at the time of their Revolution in 1776. An old Huguenot song said: "Spirit who made them live, awaken their children, so that they will know how to follow them."

Puritans and Separatists in England

God not only prepares people to shape history, but He also shapes history to prepare people so that they may fulfill their destiny and accomplish God's purposes in the earth. This latter aspect of God's principle of preparation is evident in English history of the sixteenth century. We will see God using various leaders and events to help prepare those people who would become the "Parents of the Republic of the United States of America."

William Tyndale 1494-1536

God's chief instrument in bringing about the Reformation in England was William Tyndale. Much of Tyndale's life was spent fulfilling his vision: "If God preserves my life, I will cause a boy that driveth a plow to know more of the Scriptures than the pope." Tyndale's dream was accomplished, but only at a great cost.

He spent over twelve years in exile from his native country, all the time facing the possibility of being captured and put to death. During this time, he translated the Bible from the original languages with the idea of making it available for the common man. His New Testament was published in 1525. So scholarly was Tyndale's work that is has been estimated that our present English Bibles retain eighty percent of his original work in the Old Testament, and ninety percent in the New.

In 1536 Tyndale was betrayed, arrested, and killed as a heretic. On the day of his death, Tyndale calmly stated: "I call God to record that I have never altered, against the voice of my conscience, one syllable of his Word. Nor would I this day, if all the pleasures, honors, and riches of the earth might be given to me."

Before he was strangled and burned at the stake he prayed for King Henry VIII who had persecuted and put to death many reformers and caused Tyndale to flee his country. As he was being fastened to the stake he cried out with these final words: "Lord, open the king of England's eyes!" Although his life was extinguished, the flames of liberty would burn brighter than ever, for the Word of God would be spread to all people throughout England.

During Tyndale's life many copies of his New Testament were circulated throughout England, but only under cover for the king had banned Tyndale's work. Shortly after Tyndale's death, Henry VIII "authorized the sale and the reading of the Bible throughout the kingdom", for he wanted "to emancipate England from Romish domination", and saw the "Holy Scriptures as the most powerful engine to destroy the papal system." Ironically, the king put his approval on the Matthew Bible (the revised to be called The Great Bible promoted by Henry VIII in 1539), which was in reality Tyndale's work under another name.

As the Word of God spread throughout the land, many people cried out with Tyndale, "We know that this Word is from God, as we know that fire burns; not because anyone has told us, but because a Divine fire consumes our hearts."[1]

These men and events all contribute to the movement of the Chain of Christianity and the beginning of liberty upon the earth. We will continue to trace the hand of God in history and see various links in the Chain of Christianity. As we do, "We should never forget that the prison, the scaffold, and the stake were stages in the march of civil and religious liberty which our forefathers had to travel in order that we might attain our present liberty."[2]

Henry VIII 1534

When Henry VIII became king of England in 1509, Roman Catholicism was the established religion, not only in England, but in all of Europe. The government of the church reached beyond its Biblical sphere of jurisdiction by exercising control in all areas of life.

Most people, when they hear of Henry VIII, think of his many wives. His first wife, Catherine of Aragon, had borne him no sons, plus he had acquired a particular fondness for Anne Boleyn, so he decided to divorce Catherine. Such action required permission from the pope, so Henry sent a petition asking for approval for the divorce. When he was denied approval, Henry, not being the submissive type, decided he would not only go on and divorce Catherine, but he would also divorce himself (and take England with him) from the Catholic Church.

Henry and England thus split from the Roman Catholic Church and around 1534 set up the Church of England in its place. At the time, the only difference in the two was that Henry was the pope over the Church of England instead of the Pope in Rome. However, this event would prove to be very important in the advancement of religious and civil liberty in England and throughout the world.

God was using Henry, who was not a godly man, to fulfill His purposes. Henry's actions toward Tyndale and other reformers (His policies led to Tyndale's and many others' death) reveal that his split from Rome had nothing to do with godly reform, but only selfish desires; yet, God who governs in the affairs of men, was using this historical event to accomplish His will. We saw earlier how God even used Henry to distribute Bibles that Tyndale had translated. While Henry broke from Roman Catholicism, there was still no freedom for individuals to worship God. Due to Tyndale's translation of the Bible people throughout England were being awakened, yet the climate of Henry's England did not permit reform to flourish. Many saw that the Church of England needed reform as much as the Catholic Church, but little external reform occurred under Henry.

Edward VI 1547

When Henry VIII died in 1547, he left the throne in the hands of his son, Edward VI, and Edward's protectorates. They favored those who wanted further reform in the Church of England. Under Edward the Puritan movement was born. Those people desiring to purify the Church of its errors and ungodliness were called "purifiers" or "puritans".

These reformers were overjoyed when Edward assumed power, for they could now begin to freely carry out their desired reform. Yet, they learned that one righteous ruler is not enough to ensure reform within a nation.

"Bloody" Mary 1553

Edward died in 1553, having reigned only six years. His half-sister and Henry's daughter, Mary, succeeded him to the throne. She has earned the title, *Bloody Mary,* for she put to death hundreds of reformers including the "first Puritan", John Hooper. It was Hooper who first denied the right of the State to interfere with religion in 1553.

Mary not only detested the church reforms that occurred under Edward, but also never liked the fact that her father had separated from the Catholic Church. She set about to make amends with the Pope and purge England of the Puritan movement. She caused 286 Reformed Anglican leaders, including Thomas Cranmer, Nicholas Ridley, and Hugh Larimer, to be burned at the stake.

Consequently, thousands of Puritans fled England to places in Europe that harbored reformers, and in particular, Geneva. Due to the influence of Calvin, Geneva was one of the most free and advanced cities in the world. Internal liberty, resulting from Biblical truth, was affecting all aspects of society in Geneva—from religious and civil freedom to education for the general populace and the best sanitation system in all of Europe.

It was in Geneva that the English Puritans were taught much Biblical truth that they were lacking, in particular ideas on civil liberty. God made sure that the people He was preparing were equipped in every way. He even used Bloody Mary to help accomplish His purposes.

Elizabeth I 1558

Mary died in 1558, after reigning only five years, and was succeeded by her half-sister, Elizabeth. This began the Elizabethan Era.

Elizabeth did not want England to return to Catholicism, but she also was not interested in promoting the needed reforms within the Church of England. She did promise religious toleration which caused many Puritans to return to England who had fled during Mary's reign.

As the Puritans returned, they brought with them fuller ideas of civil and religious liberty, plus the Geneva Bible. While in exile in Geneva, a number of reformers translated and published a relatively compact and affordable Bible. The Geneva Bible would become the Bible of the masses. Since it was also the first English Bible to be divided into chapter and verse, it proved to be a good study Bible.

After a few years, Elizabeth saw her tolerance of reformers was causing many to cry out for more reform than she desired, so in 1562 she issued her *Articles of Religion* which prohibited further reform. At this, some of the Puritans gave up hope of ever seeing the needed church reform and separated themselves from the Church of England. Thus, the "Separatist" movement was bora around 1580. The Pilgrims who first sailed to America in 1620 were English separatists.

The Separatist movement continued to grow throughout Elizabeth's long reign, although there were attempts from within England and from other nations to stop it.

The Miraculous Defeat of the Spanish Armada 1588

Satan hates revival and will use any means to try to stop it. The Catholic monarchs of France initiated the massacre of 30,000 Protestants (Huguenots) on St. Bartholomew's Day in 1572. Finding that persecution only strengthened the movement in England, Satan attempted to stamp it out by war.

In 1588, Philip II of Spain sent the Spanish Armada to bring England again under the dominion of Rome. A British historian of the period, Richard Hakluyt, writes of this event:

"It is most apparent, that God miraculously preserved the English nation. For the L. Admiral wrote unto her Majestie that in all humane reason, and according to the judgement of all men (every circumstance being duly considered) the English men were not of any such force, whereby they might, without a miracle dare once to approach within sight of the Spanish Fleet: insomuch that they freely ascribed all the honour of their victory unto God, who had confounded the enemy, and had brought his counsels to none effect.... While this wonderful and puissant navy was syling along the English coastes,... all people throut England prostrated themselves with humble prayers and supplications unto God: but especially the outlandish churches (who had greatest cause to feare, and against whom by name the Spaniards had threatened most grievous torments) enjoyned to their people continual fastings and supplications... knowing right well, that prayer was the onely refuge against all enemies, calamities, and necessities, and that it was the onely solace and reliefe for mankind, being visited with afflictions and misery."[3]

Here is what happened: As the Spanish fleet sailed up the English Channel, they were met by the much smaller English navy. In the natural, the English had no hope, yet all of England had been fastingand praying. A storm arose which blew many of the Spanish ships up against the coast of Holland, causing them to sink. Oddly, the smaller English ships were not affected by the storm and were able to maneuver next to the Spanish ships and set many of them on fire. A few Spanish ships limped back to Spain without touching English soil.

God had providentially intervened to protect His people and ensure that England would fulfill its purpose as a nation. Even the nation of Holland acknowledged the hand of God. In commemoration of the event, they minted a coin. On one side were ships sinking; on the other, men on their knees in prayer with the inscription: "Man Proposeth, God Disposeth," and the date "1588".

Chapter 5.
The United States, The Global South, and Liberty in Modern Times

The Separatist Movement began in England in the latter part of the sixteenth century, as people began to embrace the idea of "reformation without tarrying for any." The Separatists in and around the little town of Scrooby in the north of England wrote a church covenant—the first of its kind affirming church self-government in 1606.

One of their leaders was William Brewster was one of the only Pilgrims to have position in English society, but when the Church of England demanded more rigid conformity to its rituals and rejected the right of individuals to hear "unauthorized" preachers, Brewster finally decided to separate from the Church and to covenant with other Christians in his area to form a Scriptural congregation." Brewster later served as an elder in the congregation that left England to go to America. During the first year in America, the Pilgrims had no pastor, so Brewster effectively served in that capacity.

The Separatist pastor in England was John Robinson who joined the Separatist congregation that met in the home of William Brewster in Scrooby. He propounded religious toleration in an intolerant age and representative government in an age of absolute monarchy. For twenty years, he taught these principles in depth to his persecuted and beloved Pilgrim church. More than any other man, John Robinson prepared a people to take dominion in the new lands of today's United States to the glory of God.

One of the best known Pilgrim Fathers was William Bradford. He served as governor of their first colony in Massachusetts for 33 years and also wrote the *History of Plymouth Plantation,* the first great literary work of America. It was 1602 when Bradford started attending the Separatist Church in Scrooby and later went to America.

William Bradford's history *Of Plymouth Plantation* written in 1647 plainly reveals God's hand in the Pilgrim's lives and in the events they went through to settle in the north parts of America. We can see no greater human example of Christian character than in the lives of the Pilgrims. He wrote that:

"...a great hope & inward zeall they had of laying some good foundation...for ye propagating & advancing ye gospell of ye kingdom of Christ in those remote parts of ye world; yea, though they should be but even as stepping-stones unto others for ye performing of so great a work." He wrote how their pastor in England told them "... you are [to] become a body politick, using amongst your selves civill governmente...to be chosen by you into office of governement,.."

After 66 days at sea, in a space no larger than a volleyball court, these 102 passengers aboard the Mayflower finally reached America. Bradford wrote of a civil agreement "made by them before they came ashore, being ye first foundation of their govermente in this place; The forme was as followeth.

"In ye name of God, Amen. We whose names are underwriten,...haveing undertaken, for ye glorie of God, and advancemente of ye Christian faith...[do] solemnly & mutually in ye presence of God, and one of another, covenant & combine our selves togeather into a civill body politick...to enacte, constitute, and frame such just & equall lawes, ordinances, acts, constitutions, & offices, from time to time, as shall be thought most meete & convenient for ye generall good of ye Colonie, unto which we promise all due submission and obedience."

Although half of the group died that first winter in the new world due to disease and harsh conditions, they finally were able to grow enough food to survive. So Governor Bradford appointed a day of Thanksgiving and invited the nearby Indians to celebrate and give thanks unto God with them. Chief Massasoit and ninety of his men came and feasted with the Pilgrims. This is where the American tradition of having a holiday feast called Thanksgiving began. In the words of Bradford: "as one small candle may light a thousand, so ye light here kindled hath shone to many, yea in some sorte to our whole nation; let ye glorious name of Jehova have all ye praise."

America's Liberty and Prosperity Came from Knowing the Bible

There is a direct causal relationship between the dispersion of the Bible in the hands of the people and the rise of civil liberty. A survey of civil government from the time of Christ to the present reveals a sudden profusion of documents such as the Mayflower Compact, English Bill of Rights, and the Constitution beginning in 1620. Before this there existed only pagan monarchies.

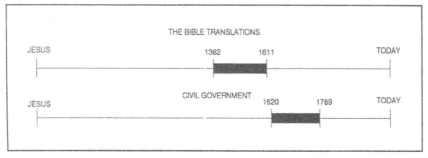

What produced these changes in ideas of government? How does one explain this? For two centuries prior to these changes, the Bible began to be translated and disseminated in the common language. It all began with John Wycliffe in 1382 who said of his new translation into English: "This Bible is for the government of the people, by the people, and for the people."[1] As people began to read the Bible, two things occurred: The church began to return to Biblical Christianity, and society began to be reformed and enjoy civil liberty.

Without the Great Awakening (1740-1760) there would have been no American Revolution (1760-1790). The ideas, the motivation, the Biblical worldview, and the great virtuous statesmanship seen in the Founder's Era were all birthed in this great revival led by Jonathan Edwards and George Whitefield. George Washington, Samuel Adams, Thomas Jefferson and others were deeply affected by the revival.

During this Great Awakening the Spirit of God swept mightly throughout the colonies. The numbers of people in the churches more than doubled. Whole towns were literally converted to Christ. Benjamin Franklin wrote in his *Autobiography* that "it seem'd as if all the world were growing religious, so one could not walk thro' the town in an evening without hearing psalms sung in different families of every street."

Many new revivalist universities were established to cultivate and propagate seeds of liberty and raise up a learned clergy. The clergy trained at these universities helped to spread Biblical principles to all the colonies. They continued to cultivate the Christian ideas of Liberty up to the Revolution.

The American Christian Revolution

The man who became known as the "Father of the Revolution"—Samuel Adams "... was a member of the church; and the austere purity of his life witnessed the sincerity of his profession. Evening and morning his house was a house of prayer; and no one more revered the Christian sabbath...."' He understood the conflict between the colonies and England was more than an economic or political struggle. He recognized, as only a Christian truly could, that the British government had violated the colonists' rights as Christians.

He worked for twenty years promoting the cause of liberty. In 1772 Samuel Adams proposed "Committees of Correspondence" to be established throughout the colonies because he desired all people to be educated in order that they could reason out their rights and political convictions based upon Biblical principles. His desire was for the colonies to be united "not by external bonds, but by the vital force of distinctive ideas and principles."[2] This unity of ideas and principles helped to promote union among the colonists. The common ideas sown within the colonists by Samuel Adams and many other Christian thinking men of that and earlier generations resulted in the external union of the colonies into the United States of America. The first letter circulated among the Colonists in 1772 was called the *Rights of the Colonists* and was written by Sam Adams himself.

England in 1774 tried to enforce an unpopular tax by blockading the port of Boston to starve them into submission. But the colonies of Massachusetts, Connecticut and Virginia called for days of fasting and prayer. One historian of that time wrote: "... large congregations filled the churches. In Virginia the members of the House of Burgesses assembled at their place of meeting; went in procession, with the speaker at their head, to the church and listened to a discourse. 'Never,' a lady wrote, 'since my residence in Virginia have I seen so large a congregation as was this day assembled to hear divine service.' The preacher selected for his text the words: 'be strong and of good courage, fear not, nor be afraid of them; for the Lord thy God, He it is that doth go with thee. He will not fail thee nor forsake thee.' 'The people,' Jefferson says, 'met generally, with anxiety and alarm in their countenances; and the effect of the day, through the whole colony, was like a shock of electricity..."

The colonies responded in material support as well, not by governmental decree but, more significantly, by individual action. A grassroots movement of zealous workers went door to door to gather patriotic offerings. This was the greatest miracle of the Revolution: Unity emerged out of Diversity. This is why *E. Pluribus Unum,* ("one from the many"), became a motto on their money even to this day. Three million people that had been previously identified with their 13 separate colonies, much like in Latin America, managed to achieve Biblical Christian Unity due to their faith, character and common worldview based on their mutual knowledge of the Bible.

Even when their delegates gathered in their first Congress, they began with prayer that last a couple hours. One of the men elected to Congress was a Presbyterian pastor named Rev. John Witherspoon, a delegate from New Jersey. As the delegates debated whether to declare independence from England or not he said: "There is a tide in the affairs of men. We perceive it now before us. To hesitate is to consent to our own slavery. That noble instrument should be subscribed to this very morning by every pen in this house. Though these gray hairs must soon descend to the sepulchre, I would infinitely rather that they descend thither by the hand of the executioner than desert at the crisis the sacred cause of my country!" When everyone agreed to independence then Samuel Adams, rose and stated: "We have this day restored the Sovereign to Whom alone men ought to be obedient. He reigns in heaven and... from the rising to the setting sun, may His kingdom come."

In all their towns, the pastors of their churches taught their people the importance of standing and fighting for Biblical principles and rights from God. Rev. David Jones preached one of the day's most eloquent sermons entitled, *Defensive War in a Just Cause Sinless.* In this sermon he appealed to the history of Israel and noted that "when vice and immorality became prevalent; when they forsook and rebelled against their God, (then) they lost their martial spirit." Then the nation experienced revival under the leadership of Nehemiah who stirred the people to arm themselves with these words: "Be not ye afraid of them: Remember the Lord, which is great and terrible, and fight for the brethren, your sons and your daughters, your wives and your houses!" Rev. Jones proved from many Scriptural examples how a defensive war is sinless before God, and when it is proper to use force against a tyrant.

J. Wingate Thornton declared in his book *The Pulpit of the American Revolution:* "Thus it is manifest, in the spirit of our history, in our annals, and by the general voice of the fathers of the republic, that, in a very great degree,—to the pulpit, the Puritan pulpit, we owe the moral force which won our independence." John Quincy Adams, one of America's early Presidents said that "The highest glory of the American

Revolution was this: it connected, in one indissoluble bond, the principles of civil government with the principles of Christianity."

Indeed in their Declaration of Independence, they said that "they are endowed by their Creator with certain unalienable rights" and went on to declare their dependence on God by "appealing to the Supreme Judge of the World" for "the protection of divine Providence."

The American Revolution was a revolution of ideas long before it was a revolution of war. And once war came, God's grace was evident in order that the world's most powerful military might be defeated. George Washington, who was commander during the war, later became the nation's first President. He took the oath of office in 1789 with his hand on a Bible opened to Deuteronomy 28, which promises blessings or curses on a nation according to its faithfulness to keep God's Word. At the end of the oath he added the words "So help me God" and leaned over and kissed the Bible because of its significance in the uniting and founding of America. He then said: "... No people can be bound to acknowledge and adore the Invisible Hand which conducts the affairs of men more than the people of the United States. Every step by which they have advanced to the character of an independent nation seems to have been distinguished by some token of providential agency...." Likewise Congress urged the people to thank God for providing us "... the light of Gospel truth..." and to ask Him to "... raise up from among our youth men eminent for virtue, learning and piety, to His service in the Church and State; to cause virtue and true religion to flourish;... and to fill the world with His glory."

Latin American Independence, the Global South, and Liberty spreading worldwide

The American nation was by no means perfect. The sinful nature of man was still at work in such institutions as slavery. The anti-slavery movement became well-organized in 1834 with one-third of its leaders being clergyman. These evangelical abolition societies eventually helped birth the Republican party in 1854. But it was too little too late. Eventually a great war emerged between the slave and free states.

President Abraham Lincoln described it best in his Second Inaugural Address:

"Both read the same Bible and pray to the same God, and each invokes His aid against the other. It may seem strange that any men should dare to ask a just God's assistance in wringing their bread from the sweat of other men's faces, but let us judge not that we be not judged. The prayer of both could not be answered. That of neither has been answered fully. The almighty has His own purposes. Woe unto the world because of offences, for it must needs be that offences come, but woe to that man by whom the offence cometh. If we shall suppose that American slavery is one of those offences which, in the providence of God, must needs come, but which having continued through His appointed time, He now wills to remove, and that He gives to both North and South this terrible war as the woe due to those by whom the offence came, shall we discern there any departure from those divine attributes which the believers in a living God always ascribe to Him? Fondly do we hope, fervently do we pray, that this mighty scourge of war may speedily pass away. Yet if God wills that it continue until all the wealth piled by the bondsman's two hundred and fifty years of unrequited toil shall be sunk, and until every drop of blood drawn with the lash shall be paid by another drawn with the sword, as was said three thousand years ago, so still it must be said, that the judgements of the Lord are true and righteous altogether."

The passion for freedom stirred in Latin America beginning with Pedro Morillo in Bolivia in 1810 and among many others in the region and led to the independence of many nations in the 1820s from Spain's control. However it would take many more years before ideas of liberty found in the Bible would spread into the mind of people enough to gradually force real freedoms to be established in those nations. Similarly, in Europe nations began to replace their monarchs with democratic governments in the mid-19th century and serfdom was abolished. And as Protestant missionaries continued to spread biblical ideas in Africa, Asia and other lands, the global south began to emerge into greater freedom. In fact, in the past 200 years over 60 countries have come into full freedom. This was something entirely new in world history that had not existed for thousands of years. The reason indirectly was the spread of Christian ideas around the globe. There are still many problems of course. Corruption, poverty and injustice is still prevalent in many countries, but it is undoubtedly a new era for the world.

The key is found in biblical best practices for every key institution of life. In Part Two we will begin to examine what the bible teaches for those important spheres of influence so that we might continue to push for greater transformation in our own city and nation.

SECTION TWO

Introduction of Section Two

The ABC's of Nations: Essential Foundations

The following chapters deal with the seven essential "mountains" of culture, i.e. the foundations and structures present in all nations. We can easily remember these by the alphabetic order as follows:
- A   Arts/Media/Entertainment
- B   Business
- C   Church
- D   Doctors (Health & Science)
- E   Education
- F   Family
- G   Government

The principles of the Bible for each area must be infused into the lives of the citizens of a nation desiring to be free, just, and prosperous. It is through the homes, educational institutions, churches, and media outlets that these principles are taught to the nation. If these institutions do not fulfill their God-given purposes and responsibilities, the citizens will lack the necessary character and understanding to support the structures of a Godly nation and the result will be bondage, injustice, and poverty.

God builds nations with individuals
It is important for us to see that God puts emphasis on individuals. Before God ever founded any institution he began the world by creating individuals and gave every individual certain duties and responsibilities to perform. These individual duties are summed up in what Jesus called the greatest commandments
1. "Love the Lord your God." (Luke 10:27, Deut. 6:5)
2. "Love your neighbor." (Luke 10:27, Lev. 19:9-18, Mt.25:35-36)

Even before there was a church God expected man to worship Him. And the love and respect of one's neighbor was part of the human mission before any church taught it or society required it. Besides these commands God added others that were the foundation of key institutions such as the family, business and government. In the next chapters we will look at these key institutions or "mountains" of culture that are the most influential for shaping the future of a nation.

Chapter 6

Church

The Mission of the Church

Jesus said in Matthew 28:20 that our mission was to preach to all creatures and *"make disciples of all nations"* by the method of *"teaching them to observe all things whatsoever I have commanded you."* In the historic church that transformed pagan Europe into a Christian culture, we have evidence in history of how they understood their mission. They did not start building places of worship for several centuries. Their primary focus was on building people who were like ambassadors of another kingdom in every neighborhood, workplace and civic activity.

The main purpose and responsibilities of pastors and church leadership can be summarized from Scripture and church history as follows:

First, to gather the people of God for **worship** and the Lord's Supper (1 Cor 5:8-13; 11:23-25).

Second, to **instruct** God's people in Biblical truth for every sphere of life, not just religious topics (2 Tim 3:16-17).

Third, to **equip and mobilize God's people for service**, not just in the church, but in all the other key areas of life where believers spend most of their lives in their own callings, i.e. the other six cultural "mountains" (Eph 4:11-12,16; Titus 3:8,14).

Many pastors today may indeed feel they do these three things but usually this is not so. The second item, to instruct believers, is often limited to personal piety and church life, And the third item, to equip and mobilize believers for service is too often only for church ministry, rather than for their calling in the workplace, the marketplace or civic life. These other areas are too often thought of as worldly, or at least less important than church activity and therefore real commitment to train, organize and mobilize church members for these things rarely happens. At best the pastors might tolerate and announce activities of those "activists" among them, but rarely does church leadership actually empower and highlight these things from the pulpit and directly support them.

Often today the measurement of success for a pastor is if there is increasing numbers of members (and a mega-church is deemed superior), and construction of their own facilities. Along with that is the number of church activities and events (even though almost all are religious activities and rarely related to transforming culture outside the church). But in the New Testament those measurements of success are non-existent. Jesus himself and all of the Apostles would have been considered a failure by this criteria. None built a church building and their members were relatively small in number.

But when Jesus gave the mission to go preach, baptize and "make disciples of all the nations" He went on to also give them criteria for measuring themselves. In the parallel passage of the Great Commission found in Mark 16 Jesus added "signs" that would follow this mission. In other words, there was a way to measure progress of evangelism and discipling nations. He gave them measurable goals as follows:
1. "cast out demons"
2. "lay hands on the sick and they will recover"
3. "speak in new tongues"
4. "take up serpents and not be harmed"

Most people read these things in purely a personal manner, but since they followed Christ's reference to "nations" then these signs should be applied to the larger mission as well. Indeed when doing so, they become even more interesting. Let us examine these more closely.

Cast Out Demons.
The first way a church can measure itself is the degree to which it is effectively dealing with the spiritual forces of darkness over not just individuals, but whole people groups and culture. Jesus once told the disciples He saw satan fall from heaven as they were preaching the Word of God. Paul later taught the Ephesians of the battle they do against "principalities and powers in the heavenly

places" and to the Corinthians he told them of the need to tear down strongholds with the weapons that are might through God. This perhaps is already something churches may do through preaching and prayer meetings. Informed intercession in unity with other churches in a region is essential to see darkness pushed back and breakthrough come. Many good books are already available on this and the reader is encouraged to seek those out.

Lay Hands On the Sick

A second way a church can measure itself is the degree to which it is dealing with sickness not only in individuals but in culture. Not only are individuals sick, but also nations. In 2 Chronicles 7:14 God told Israel that *"If My people who are called by My name will humble themselves, and pray and seek My face, and turn from their wicked ways, then I will hear from heaven, and will forgive their sin and heal their land."* Notice the need for their land to be healed. To heal a nation, governments are inadequate. U.N. peacekeepers can be sent into a situation to stop bloodshed but they can never heal any root cause of the violence. God said that it only the "people who are called by my name" that can heal nations.

But to heal a nation it requires that God's people "lay hands on the sick." This means that prayer meetings will not do it. It takes personal engagement with those who are hurting. This can mean practical hands-on care of people with physical sicknesses, with compassionate health care. Historically the church has been on the cutting edge of medicine, using medical missions to open new closed nations to the gospel, and opening closed hearts in the inner cities or remote lands in their own nations.

But it also means reaching out across cultural and ethnic walls to heal racial divisions and other hurts from prejudice and disputes that have simmered perhaps centuries long. Like the parable Jesus told of the "good Samaritan" (Luke 10:29-37), it takes courage and effort to get into the ditch to help people who are different from us and with whom our friends and culture often tells us to avoid. But he did so, and probably not only got criticized but also got dirty and bloody in the process. He sacrificed of his own finances as well. This is what it takes for the church to heal a nation – it has to reach and touch those ugly things that others will not. It takes the "laying on of hands" to see reconciliation and healing come to a culture. But this is a second clear criteria to measure our faithfulness to the Great Commission of Christ. It is a "sign" that we are doing our job well.

Speak In New Tongues

A third way a church can measure itself is the degree to which it is speaking in new tongues, not just in one's prayer closet or church gathering, but in the culture. When Jesus spoke these words, the disciples had never experienced Pentecost and had only one context of Scripture to comprehend Jesus' teaching. By giving a mission of discipling nations and mentioning speaking in tongues, the disciples would easily associate it with the story in Genesis 11 when that once occurred:

> *Now the whole earth had one language and one speech. And it came to pass, as they journeyed from the east, that they found a plain in the land of Shinar, and they dwelt there. Then they said to one another, "Come, let us make bricks and bake them thoroughly." They had brick for stone, and they had asphalt for mortar. And they said, "Come, let us build ourselves a city, and a tower whose top is in the heavens; let us make a name for ourselves, lest we be scattered abroad over the face of the whole earth." But the LORD came down to see the city and the tower which the sons of men had built. And the LORD said, "Indeed the people are one and they all have one language, and this is what they begin to do; now nothing that they propose to do will be withheld from them. Come, let Us go down and there confuse their language, that they may not understand one another's speech." So the LORD scattered them abroad from there over the face of all the earth, and they ceased building the city. Therefore its name is called Babel, because there the LORD confused the language of all the earth; and from there the LORD scattered them abroad over the face of all the earth.*

In order to stop the scheme of their political leader Nimrod to centralize political power, God caused the people to "speak in new tongues." In Gen 10:8-10 Nimrod was described as the first "mighty one in the earth" meaning a dictator who was the first to established a kingdom in human history. All ancient pagan civilizations adopted the same style of totalitarian monarchy. But God's intervention at Babel was an act of love to protect people from abuse. Their leaders were using the nationalistic pride of the people ("to make a name for ourselves") to promise them construction projects that would be greater than any on earth, if the people would give of their resources, time and labor to support the goal. The centralization of power is always the pagan solution for solving problems, but almost always leads to more problems and loss of liberty. Centralization is dangerous and therefore God intervenes in human history (i.e. "the Lord came down") and thwarts it here by making them speak in new tongues. It was an act that turned the culture back more to God's decentralized model of life.

This was the sign that Jesus said should be evident in the disciples' ministry in their own nations. They should be used by God as effective communicators of a message quite different from the world's model of culture – one that empowered all people instead of one or a few at the top. The language that was given to the church to liberate nations was the one found in the Bible. When its truths are declared by the church into the culture, it often unites people for good and defeats the forces of evil that are at work in the free marketplace of ideas.

To speak God's tongue in a culture the church must learn the worldview of the Bible for all of life and learn to speak it in a way that is relevant to even unbelievers. They must learn to speak its truth without having to quote chapter and verse and make it plain in language that anyone can appreciate. They must then take it outside of religious circles and into the culture using every means of communication possible. This means to use every avenue of education and media and the arts. This is a third clear criteria to measure our faithfulness to the Great Commission of Christ. It is a "sign" that we are really doing our mission and not just doing religious activity.

Take Up Serpents

A fourth way a church can measure itself is the degree to which it is confronting and seizing the dangerous things in the culture. When Jesus gave a mission of discipling nations and mentioned taking up serpents, the disciples would easily associate it with the story in Exodus 3:9-10; 4:2-4 when God previously sent Moses to confront a powerful political leader:

> *Now therefore, behold, the cry of the children of Israel has come to Me, and I have also seen the oppression with which the Egyptians oppress them. Come now, therefore, and I will send you [Moses] to Pharaoh that you may bring My people, the children of Israel, out of Egypt." [When Moses expressed doubt]....the LORD said to him, "What is that in your hand?" He said, "A rod." And He said, "Cast it on the ground." So he cast it on the ground, and it became a serpent; and Moses fled from it. Then the LORD said to Moses, "Reach out your hand and take it by the tail" (and he reached out his hand and caught it, and it became a rod in his hand)."*

Since Moses grew up in Pharoah's house he knew just how powerful this man was. The Egyptian tyrant was leader of perhaps the greatest military on earth at that time. No one could make demands of Pharoah and survive. When God miraculously turned Moses' staff into a serpent Moses was afraid of it. His natural mind told him to keep distance in order to be safe. When God then told him to "take it" he had to make a decision to trust God's word over his own natural thinking. When he did, Moses learned he could also trust God to protect him from this powerful human leader.

In the governments of the nations both in history and modern times, we find the gathering place of many "serpents." Politics is a dirty and dangerous business and the Christian is often told to keep their distance. But if good people stay away from government then it guarantees that evil triumphs. It never changes. In 1916 Rev. Charles Aked said it well that **"for evil men to accomplish their purpose it is only necessary that good men should do nothing." (A quote wrongly attributed to Edmund Burke).** It takes the courageous efforts of righteous people to break the power of evil in the governments and politics of the nations.

But this is a fourth clear criteria to measure our faithfulness to the Great Commission. It is a "sign" that we are doing our job well when good people get involved in politics and those areas where evil has great sway and begins to push back the darkness in the highest places of the nation. One thing is for sure: if Christians do everything else, evangelism, reconciliation, prayer, mercy ministry, education, communications, etc, but avoid the political and business realms where the greatest snakes are, that nation will never be completely transformed or fully discipled as Christ commanded.

Pastors have to measure themselves differently. Regardless of size, are their churches producing people who are not only interceding against demonic powers, but also healing the culture, communicating to the culture, and confronting the corrupt leadership of the culture? These are the signs that should be following our work.

Teaching All That I Commanded

In the great commission Jesus gave to pastors the primary method of their work: education. They themselves are not the ones that have to become involved in politics or media or schools or reconciliation and medicine. Nothing is wrong if they do, but their main task according to Ephesians 4:12 is to equip the saints for the work of the ministry. In other words, when a church's leadership faithfully is "teaching them all that I commanded" then transformation of a nation is possible. What does this mean practically? A church must expand its Sunday sermons and discipleship programs beyond the exclusive focus of individual salvation and personal piety and victory in life. Many churches include in the bible classes and small-group curriculum a focus on family, which is good. Some churches also have some teaching on work and business. But the curriculum should eventually include all of the six key areas of influence in culture. Family, Business, Education, Media, Health Care, and Government. This can be done gradually of course. [Note: In this book we do not have a chapter on the area of medicine, but you may find this in our other series of book.] A model of discipleship is illustrated below.

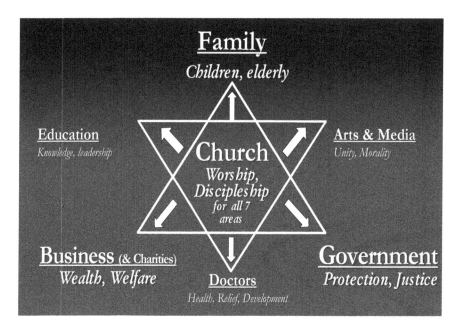

The illustration shows the church in the center as the place where people are trained in a biblical worldview for all of the other areas. The diagram might make the reader think of the star of David and the nation of Israel. Israel of course was Gods' chosen nation but if any modern nation has the people of God learning and leading in all of these areas, then their nation may also be blessed by God. That is Christ's Great Commission vision – go and disciple all the nations!

Why The Influence of Christianity is weak in a nation

An early American pastor, Dr. Jedidiah Morse, preached an insightful Election Sermon in 1799 from the Biblical text: "If the foundations be destroyed, what can the righteous do?" (Psalm 11:3). He said:

> To the kindly influence of Christianity we owe that degree of civil freedom, and political and social happiness which mankind now enjoys. In proportion as the genuine effects of Christianity are diminished in any nation, either through unbelief or the corruption of its doctrine, or the neglect of its institutions; in the same proportion will the people of

that nation recede from the blessings of genuine freedom, and approximate the miseries of complete despotism....

He said that the "genuine effects of Christianity are diminished in any nation" through (1) unbelief, (2) corruption of its doctrines, and (3) neglect of its institutions. Let us look briefly at each of these.

Unbelief

"And how shall they believe in Him whom they have not heard? And how shall they hear without a preacher?" (Romans 10:14). A nation cannot be blessed without strong vibrant churches. These cannot exist without dedicated godly preachers. This by no means requires a majority of the population to be converted to be a godly nation. Rarely in history has there been a majority of genuine believers, but if a committed minority really understand their duties in all of life, they can shape a nation. But revival and awakening of the lost is essential to grow at least a strong core of the population that follows Christ and his teaching.

Corruption of Doctrine

The doctrine that this refers to has nothing to do with your typical "statement of faith" that most Christians hold to as essential fundamentals. Those doctrines are generally confined to religious questions concerning the Godhead, salvation, etc. The doctrines that, when corrupted or neglected results eventually in the weakness of Christianity in society, were understood well by the apostles. These are articulated well in a sermon by Paul the apostle in Acts 17:24-28:

> The God who made the world and all things in it since he is Lord of heaven and earth does not dwell in temples made with hands; neither is He served by human hands, as though He needed anything, since He Himself gives to all life and breath and all things; and He made from one, every nation of mankind to live on all the face of the earth, having determined their appointed times, and the boundaries of their habitation that they should seek God, if perhaps they might grope for Him and find Him, though He is not

far from each one of us; for in Him we live and move and exist.

Four primary doctrines that have practical implications on how we view the world are mentioned here:

(1) Creation — "God made the world."
It didn't just happen by chance. When this doctrine is not taught in a reasonable way, then Christians will began to neglect the field of science. Creation will become an irrelevant "religious" dogma. This neglect leaves a void for a competing ideology — Evolution. Charles Darwin wrote his book in 1859, but it never really became predominant in public education until a lack of biblical scientific reasoning became the norm. Today, the tables are being turned, as Creation Scientists are restoring solid reasoning for Christians to articulate rather than simply saying, "the Lord made the earth."

(2) Lordship — "He is Lord of Heaven and earth."
This means He is absolute master and final authority to whom all must give allegiance. As this doctrine has been neglected, so another competing ideology has gained the ascendancy—secular humanism. This says that man is the measure of all things and the one who determines right and wrong for himself.

(3) Providence—"He Himself gives to all life and breath and all things; . . .for in Him we live and move and exist."
Truly God is the source of everyman's provisions, to Whom each man and woman must look. As this doctrine has been neglected, so the competing ideology of socialism has prospered. The socialistic ideas promulgated in Karl Marx's book, written in 1844, will not have much influence where Christians live and preach biblical principles of economics. Also, a lack of Christian character tends to allow

greed and materialism to grow and wealth to be accumulated instead of compassionately employed to meet the needs of the poor and society. Individual interests replace the common good of the community. These needs are then exploited by Marxist and Socialist leaders.

(4) Sovereignty—"He made . . . every nation . . . having determined their
appointed times and the boundaries of their habitation."

When God's sovereignty is not taught in schools and popular culture the ideology of existentialism will prevail. Existentialists believe history is meaningless and the future unpredictable. Therefore to plan and work for goals is hopeless. Their philosophy is "Eat, drink, and be merry for tomorrow we die." It is totally present-oriented and hedonistic. Even Christians subconsciously adopt the existential view of history when they focus on just awaiting heaven. They lack a sense of responsibility for the past and fail to plan for the future and are focused only on self-improvement. In the past 100 years Christians started seeing Satan as the sovereign of this world, and Jesus as an absentee king who is concerned exclusively with building and maintaining His church until He returns to earth.

The worldview of the Protestant reformers of the 16th century was diametrically opposite to this view. They saw Jesus Christ as the ruler of the earth (1 Timothy 6:16; Hebrews 2:14) and Satan as a defeated foe (John 12:3, Colossians 2:15). The God of the Bible was seen as sovereign over men and their property. This is important as a Christian writer explains below. If you believe God rules the earth:

> "1. Your commission is to subdue the earth and build godly nations through evangelizing and discipleship.
> "2. You see Christian culture as leavening all areas of life, replenishing the earth, and blessing all mankind.
> "3. All of God's world is His and every activity, to be seen as a spiritual work of God.

"4. Reformation is expected if a nation is obedient to God's word."

But if you believe Satan rules the earth:

"1. Your commission is just to concentrate on saving souls from this evil world.

"2. You see Christian culture as a counter-culture, an isolated, persecuted minority in an evil world.

"3. Church activity is primary and spiritual, while worldly pursuits are secular and to be dealt with only as a necessity.

"4. Reformation is impossible since things must get worse because Satan is in control."

Ideas truly determine consequences, and to the degree Christians have abdicated their leadership role and denied the 'crown rights of Jesus Christ,' to that degree the church loses its influence. The Christian must embrace these historical doctrines, and hold to a providential view of history such as once held in the historic church. Christianity can only be strong if there is the restoration of biblical Christianity and its teaching of practical theology, and biblical reasoning in all areas of life.

Neglect of Institutions

If the church in a society neglects the educational, economic, social, and political institutions, then those people who lack Christian character and thinking will begin to assume control of these areas. If Christians lead in only the church but let people with pagan worldview and ungodly character lead the other six key areas of cultural influence (i.e. the "mountains"), then the church will always be struggling in that nation. As these institutions are operated upon a worldly philosophy, they will not provide liberty and justice for all, but will cause the nation at large to come short of God's best. As Christians commit themselves to be the "salt of the earth," corruption will subside, "the righteous will be in authority," and "the people will rejoice" (Proverbs 29:2). "Righteousness exalts a nation" (Pr. 14:34). But Christianity will not have much impact if there is not Christian leaders seeking the **reformation of all society**.

Summary of Action Steps

But somewhere along the way, churches stopped having the nation as their mission. They began to focus just on leadership for the church itself and began to build big churches instead of big people. Churches must begin once again to provide a regular program of discipleship for their members, either through a weekly class for adults or through home-groups or special study groups that are set up for this purpose in the congregation. Near election times or around special community events and national holidays, special sermons should also be preached. These election and commemorative sermons can be preached on Sundays at church or at special
seminars for the general community. Distributing these sermons in printed form will help disseminate the truth. In addition to this, the church should try to help supplement the schooling efforts of parents by starting private schools or by coordinating special tutoring and events for home-schooling parents. Clergy should also be seeking to develop relationships with community leaders in the government, business, and media spheres so as to provide consultation and advice from a biblical perspective.

Chapter 7

Family

You Shall Teach Them…in Your Home

The national data in the United States is shocking. Studies now show that about 80% of children raised in Christian families that take them to church regularly all their lives, are dropping out of church and no longer claiming a personal faith by the time they are adults out on their own. This statistic holds true for both children of Christian families that send them to public schools and private schools. But the ONLY variable is among home-schooled children. Only about 20% of them stop being active Christians when they are adults. A remarkable 80% of them remain true to the faith of their parents even when they are on their own as adults.

Children whose parents have remained the center of their universe are different. All other kids attend church, are involved with Church youth groups, and some even in Christian schools, but the one thing that is different is that they are mostly with their peers all day long five days a week. This shifts the orientation of their decisions away from what their Christian parents had hoped for them. The results are devastating the to the American church today. The problem is that virtually every church is in denial. They think it's not going to happened to their kids. Their family and youth group and church life is probably better. Look at all these children here who seem to be benefiting and enjoying it. But the problem is that the ones who fall away are not there. Out of sight, out of mind. The kids don't usually drop out while at home, but once they move out, away at college or working their job elsewhere. No one in the local church notices and the self-deception continues unabated. But 80% of those children they see running around the church today will leave the faith. From every church. It's like a frog that is being cooked so slowly it doesn't know it until too late. The definition of insanity is to keep doing the same thing and expect to get different results. The American church is not only in denial, it's crazy.

But a new movement is emerging. What some are calling the 4 to 14 Window has become the focus of multiple global summits of Christian leaders. I have had the privilege to serve as a facilitator in many of these summits. Some leaders are beginning to say we must be brutally honest because we are losing our kids. The home-schooling movement is one of the few things that is reversing the trend. Churches, parents and teachers are starting to wake up and think outside the box.

The family "box" of modern America and indeed so much of modern western civilization is so completely different from the best practices of the historic church. Home-schooling was what Abraham and families of Israel did for over a thousand years. Then the early Christians, with roots in Israel, followed the same pattern as they spread their faith throughout the Roman Empire in Europe and beyond. They didn't send their kids to the pagan Roman schools. They raised their kids the Biblical way. And besides home-schooling their own kids, the church families banded together to start additional schools for kids of pagan families as well as for orphans and the poor. The pagans could see the Christian kids had better results and eventually this was how Christianity conquered the Roman Empire. Within three centuries half the population of the empire were identified as Christian.

The Home Is the Primary Place of Education

Parents are commanded by God to "teach" their children (Deut 6:4-7). Jewish children were taught in the home until age eight. Then some of them, as a supplement to home training, were tutored by the Levites and priests until approximately 13 years old (Gal. 4; 2 Chron 17:7-9). They were taught to read at age five. In pagan countries children received education only if they were children of royalty or elite classes, and it usually occurred outside of the home by the state.

But the state is never given this responsibility anywhere in the Bible. Never. The only mention of state education in the Bible is in Daniel, where as exiles God's people find themselves in Babylon and forced to have their youth in the pagan schools. God condemns this education and some parents sought to be exempt (see Dan. 1:3-6). Biblically, the state is given the responsibility to protect and defend its citizens, but only parents have the responsibility before God to educate their children.

If aspects of the child's education are delegated by parents to others, it is still the responsibility of the parents to seek out good tutors or schools that will do the job in the same manner they would, to "train them up in the way they should go." This means in a Biblical worldview and in godly morals. If a state school really can do that then it may be an option for the Christian parent to consider, but if there is any doubt, parents should avoid it for they will give an account to God in the end. All too often parents take the risk and hope for the best but to risk an eternal soul in one's charge is an extremely foolish gamble.

Education is an important jurisdictional responsibility of the family. The Bible teaches that the home is the primary institution for training the future generations. God chose Abraham to be a father of nations because he knew he would be faithful in this responsibility (Genesis 18:19). The father, mother and grandparents are all to take part in the education of the youth.

Ephesians 6:1-4 tells us that the **father** is especially important in the education of children. Verse 4 says: "Fathers, provoke not your children to wrath: but bring them up in the nurture and admonition of the Lord." The word nurture means "to train, to educate, to tutor; to personally have input in a child." Fathers must take time to personally train and educate their children, but at the very least the father serves as the "principal" that oversees the family's school.

A primary role of **mothers** is to teach (Proverbs 1:8; Titus 2:3). The chapter in Proverbs that has taught multitudes the characteristics of a virtuous woman was written by a man, King Lemuel, but he learned of this ideal from his own mother (Proverbs 31). Among a woman's most influential things she could ever do in life is the raising of the leaders of a nation. The 19th century American statesman Daniel Webster said that "in a free republic woman performs her sacred duty and fulfills her destiny" in a way that cannot be overestimated. He said that in the home: *The mothers of a civilized nation...work, not on frail and perishable materials, but on the immortal mind, molding and fashioning beings who are to exist forever. They work, not upon the canvas that shall perish, or the marble that shall crumble into dust, but upon mind, upon spirit,* *which is to last forever, and which is to bear, for good or evil, throughout its duration, the impress of a mother's . . . hand.* An early American pioneer in education said: "*woman is inevitably a teacher. . . . [and] should be held in the highest honor. They are the allies of legislators. They have agency in the prevention of crime. . . . Demand of her as a debt the highest excellence of which she is capable of attaining. Summon her to abandon selfish motives and inglorious ease. Incite her to those virtues which promote the permanence and health of nations. Make her accountable for the character of the next generation. Give her solemn charge in the presence of men and of angels. Gird her with the whole armor of education and piety, and see if she be not faithful to her children, to her country, and to her God . . .*"

Grandparents may also take part in the education of the youth (Deut 4:9). Timothy attributes his Christian education to his mother and grandmother (2 Tim. 1:5; 3:14-17) since his father was a pagan (Acts 16:3). Teaching by grandparents not only benefits their grandchildren but it also is a help to themselves in having purpose in their senior years. Over the years they have acquired much wisdom and knowledge that the youth need.

Why Did He Make Them One?

But there is another aspect of the family "box" that modern Christians today do differently from the ancient Hebrews and historic Christians. The first command in Genesis to married couples was to have children. In Genesis 1 God said that parents should "be fruitful and multiply." In other words, to have kids (and not just one!).

The ancient pagan world limited the number of their children by practicing some form of birth control and by practicing abortion and infanticide. While the pagan families remained static in the population the Hebrews and later the Christians grew to form the majority of the populations in the countries where they lived. In Egypt the enslaved Hebrews were told to even kill their newborn sons, but disobeyed. In exile in Babylon the prophet Jeremiah sent the strategy to the Jewish families: "Marry and have sons and daughters; find wives for your sons and give your daughters in marriage, so that they too may have sons and daughters. Increase in number there; do not decrease. Also, seek the peace and prosperity of the city to which I have carried you into exile. Pray to the LORD for it, because if it prospers, you too will prosper." (Jeremiah 29:6-7) Their false prophets told them not to because they would soon be going back to Israel. Today there are some who say that Christians should not be having many kids so they can be free to reach as many people as possible before the return of Christ.

But the historic biblical command given in the garden to mankind has never been altered: To married couples He commanded them to "multiply" (Gen 1:28). This was the foundation of the family institution. This was the primary reason that Adam needed a wife. He could take dominion as a single man but he could never "multiply." He needed Eve for that part of his mission. The words "family" and "marriage" are not found in the first chapters of the Bible but when the command to multiply was first given by God, the institution of the family came into being. They were human responsibilities, not just for Christians, but are essential best-practices that must be modeled rightly by Christians for the world to work as the Creator intended.

The reason God "hates" divorce as stated in Malachi 2 is that it destroys the ability for a family to raise "godly seed" for His kingdom. Marriage has benefits involving companionship, intimacy and sexual pleasure, but the main purpose of marriage is children. When Christians today approach marriage with primarily their own happiness and benefits in mind then they start on a wrong foundation. Often even Christians who make their own happiness the purpose of marriage, once they find themselves unhappy for whatever reason, begin to consider divorce. The purpose of the marriage is gone in their mind. But not to God. Marriage is really something that primarily exists to create a permanent secure environment for the raising of the next generation. This is why homosexual marriage is wrong. It cannot produce a child, much less, can it properly raise a child in the way they should go. But likewise heterosexual couples who never seek to have children (there are some of course who cannot biologically do so, which is a different matter) or who seek to put it off while they pursue their own happiness and vocational and material happiness pervert God's purposes for "making them one" (Malachi 2). Or if they just have one or two children, they short circuit and deny the "best practices" of the biblical and historical church. And it doesn't even make any sense to a Christian. God said in Psalm 127 that children are a reward of the Lord and are like arrows in one's hand and he who "has a quiver full" is blessed. Indeed arrows were weapons of war. Who in their right mind goes into a fight deliberately choosing to limit the number of weapons in their arsenal? But Christian families today are doing this very thing, contrary to the practice of the church in transforming nations for millennia. But when is the last time your church taught the apostolic word in 1 Timothy 5:14 for women to "…marry, bear children, manage the house, give no opportunity to the adversary to speak reproachfully"?

The modern situation is in fact frightening in some countries today. In much of the western world, especially Europe and Japan, etc, the fertility rate has dropped to below replacement levels. That means that in most of Europe for example, the total population in about 50 years from today will be roughly one third less than it is now. It is a self-made holocaust. And it will have horrendous consequences in a shrinking economy and tax-base and therefore in shrinking budgets of governments that have promised the aging population so much. It could lead to serious instability and crises of a magnitude that will have no short-term solution. Like the black plague that came to Europe, it will take generations of backwardness before it can recover. Meanwhile the southern hemisphere that is still having babies will become the dominant economies and therefore the dominant political powers in world affairs. Another shocking reality for Europe is that the only families that are really growing today are Muslims. This means that in about 50 years most of Europe will be majority Muslim nations. The historic "Christian" culture will be no more. Sharia law and so much more will become the dominant law and culture of Europe, along with nuclear weapons and industries that are now in place.

This may seem hopeless but in reality it is a great opportunity for the church if it will return to the best practices for the family that it once practiced long ago. When Christians first came to Europe they were but a fraction of one percent of the population. But by having a long-term family-based strategy, they gradually took over. Europe does not have to become a Muslim majority culture. True Christians in Europe today are but a tiny percent of the population once again but they can return to the same practices of their earliest churches and they could be the majority of Europe in 50 years themselves! This is without religious revival and awakening that sweeps many more unbelieving adults into the church. Christians must renounce the me-centered marriage and easy no-fault divorce culture for the sake of the kingdom of God on earth.

Worse than an Infidel

Another modern family "box" that is contrary to the historic Christian best practice is in regards to the care of one's elderly family members.

God commanded Israel to have the firstborn child to take care of the elderly parents and for the parents to give them a "double portion" of their inheritance to help them do this task. Likewise, in the early church, an extremely strong emphasis was made on the family taking care of their own. The issue came up in Paul's letter to Timothy regarding whether a church should take care of the elderly. Paul said in 1 Timothy 5:4, *"But if any widow has children or grandchildren, let them first learn to show piety at home and to repay their parents; for this is good and acceptable before God."* In other words the family is primarily responsible and the church only should step in if there is no other option.

But goes on to state in verse 8: *"But if anyone does not provide for his own, and especially for those of his household, he has denied the faith and is worse than an unbeliever."* Strong words. The family's role in caring for its elderly members is not an option.

Today many cultures have turned to the state to take care of seniors. But Christians should be at least the one place that preserves the family's role in this, and with the church stepping to help for all those elderly people who have no family to do so. It is worth noting that if parents have more than one child and "multiply" as God commanded, then there very rarely are going to be situations where children are not around when the parents are old. Obedience in the multiplication responsibility can bring blessing in the retirement period of life. But when parents do not do so, the one child may themselves have health issues or circumstances that prevents them from caring for their parents. Have more children and have a greater safety net in old age. This was the Biblical "social security" plan.

The family is the basic building block of society. God gave it the unique purpose of creating and educating the kids of a nation, and of caring for its seniors. The family was intended by God to be the education and social security/retirement departments of a nation. The government was never commanded in the Bible to provide these things.

The Foundation of a Free Nation Rests in the Home

As is the family in a nation, so is the church, state, education, business, arts, and life of that nation. The home is the first sphere of society and not only determines the foundation of these components of society, but also determines the extent to which they prosper.

A marriage is to be a model of the relationship between Christ and His bride the Church. Many principles for marital life are found in Scripture and must be taught. But since there are already so many great books and materials on that subject, we will not discuss that further here. Our focus will especially be on the role of the family in the nation.

The critical goal of the Christian home in a republic is to love and nurture the young, build individual character, and train future generations to govern the earth. It is here that individuals first learn the outworking of their faith and put into practice the biblical principles that support free nations. There is no single element which contributes more significantly to the success of Christian Constitutional government than the family. It is in the home where the foundations of Christian character are laid. It is in the home where Christian self-government is learned and practiced.

As Christians seek to reform the nations, they must never underestimate the importance of the family in the life of the nations. In no area should greater attention be paid than to the nature, responsibilities, duties, and influences of the home. The beginning of preparing the way for Christ to gain preeminence in a nation includes turning "the hearts of the fathers back to their children, and the hearts of the children to their fathers" (Malachi 4:6, Luke 1:17), the lack of
which brings a curse upon the land.

Parents must realize that they are equipping their children for temporal life on earth **and** for life eternal. Lack of proper training will cause those in later life to look back at their youthful home with sorrow.

The primary duties of a Christian home are to teach the Bible, seek God in prayer and worship, maintain discipline, build Christian character, and impart a biblical view of life, for if we train our children rightly, they will not depart from it (Proverbs 22:6).

If parents see children as playthings or burdens and relegate their up-bringing to others, then parental duty cannot be fulfilled. There is no substitute for the parents in this mission — no day-care, school, person, or institution can take the place of Mom or Dad.

As the Family Goes...

The family has an awesome role in a nation. To produce children who will contribute to the economy and growth of the nation, and to educate the next generation of its leaders, and to provide for its seniors are things of great consequence. It is the department of education and welfare for a nation.

But when the state takes over these functions the family especially loses its importance. The United States became one of the greatest powers on earth because of its families. But after the Civil War in America (1861-1865) a huge shift began. So many families lost their fathers economic ability to provide due to death or disability in that conflict, so mothers were forced to enter the workplace in large numbers. This meant they could no longer stay at home and be the teachers of their own children, so there was a new demand for schools outside the home. On top of this there were millions of newly-freed black families that had uneducated parents who were unable to teach their children at home. This was too overwhelming of demand for the church alone to solve, so the state stepped in to launch government public schools on a massive scale. Gradually it became the norm for all children to enter the free public schools. But this then created a new era where mothers no longer had the high calling of education filling their daily routine at home. Their sense of importance waned and thus it was logical for them to begin seeking purpose and fulfillment outside home. The feminist movement made more sense to them as they had relative insignificance at home. To be a homemaker at that point was portrayed as a life of ease yet boredom and waste of talent. As women entered the workforce in larger numbers incomes of families went up dramatically with two-income earners per household and free education for their kids. But the price was the gradual loss of a Biblical worldview in the culture and the rise of the peer group socializing children in a way that was contrary to the values of the parents. The idea of courtship under the wise protection of the family began to wane as kids just pursued romantic relationships in a modern unsupervised "dating" model. Eventually all of this led to rebellion on increasingly-coed college campuses, and thus more sex outside of marriage. With this also came more faulty marriages and an increase in divorce and adoption of easy no-fault divorce. Later followed more living together without any marriage commitment and abortion to deal with the expected pregnancies and uncommitted spouses to care for children. With the divorce culture came so-many single parent families unable to give children healthy role models from both genders and thus gave rise to sexual identify confusion, homosexuality, as well as increasing poverty and crime. In fact the single biggest indicator of crime, poverty, and immorality is the breakdown of the family. The greatest threat to the traditional family is not the gay-rights movement, it's the failure of the church to deal with divorce even among Christians. When Christians treat marriage as something primarily based on "love" and for their own pleasure and benefit instead of primarily for the raising of children, then why should homosexual couples think differently? Christians appear to them as simply bigots who want to deny benefits to others who "love" each other.

    The way back for America and Europe and other developed nations is through the family. Likewise for any country to go forward it must follow the best practices of the family in a nation as taught in the bible and modeled by the historic Christian church. Having kids, taking responsibility for their schooling, and providing for the elderly.

Chapter 8

Higher Education

The Role of the Church in Education

The Church also has a role in education as an extension of the family's responsibility for their own children but also as part of its mission to reach all the world, even the children of the unsaved. As the Church goes into all the world to disciple the nations, an integral part of this will involve education (Mt. 28:18-20). Education of the common man has accompanied the spread of the gospel in history.

Deuteronomy 6 reveals that it is the family's responsibility to educate their children but God commanded ancient Israel to be sure that every child in the nation learned the law because the success of their nation depended upon each person knowing and living the truth of God's Word. So Christians historically have also led the way in forming schools for everyone. Early Christians saw it as their responsibility to educate the general public. The Great Commission of Matthew 28:19-20, to "disciple the nations" was to be accomplished by "teaching them to observe all that I commanded you." History shows that education always accompanies the spread of the gospel.

In the first centuries of the Christian era, the Christian homes adopted the Jewish model of education for their own kids, but also started schools for unsaved children. By the Middle Ages there were still many children lacking education. John Wycliffe of England translated the Scriptures in common English in 1382, and his itinerant preachers known as Lollards distributed them. They then began to teach the people how to read so they could learn the Scriptures. Prior to this, only priests and noblemen could read the Bible. Education of the common man also followed the preaching of Luther, Tyndale, Calvin, and other Reformation preachers. The desire to educate every individual accompanied the Pilgrims,

Puritans, Quakers, and most other settlers who came to America. This idea of education for the common man was of Christian origin.

Schools were established in early America mainly because the colonists wanted their children to be able to read Scripture. These parents saw that it was not the government's but their responsibility to provide education. For the first 200 years of America's history, education was primarily centered in the home. Home education was sometimes supplemented by tutors or schools, but even here the responsibility and bulk of a child's education rested in the home.

The model of education in Colonial America was very similar to the model used by ancient Israel. Parents did it all until children were around the age of eight or nine. At this age, some children had tutors to further instruct them, or an even smaller number attended a school. With the Israelites, the Levites and the Priests were the tutors; with colonial Americans, the ministers were generally the tutors. If there were too many children in the minister's community for him to go into each home to tutor, he would receive a group of children into his home. This would comprise a child's education until around age thirteen or so when they would enter an apprenticeship program or possibly enroll in a college.

The philosophy of education in one generation will be the philosophy of government in the next generation.

Tyranny is the result of ignorance. A nation of well-informed citizens who have been taught to value their God-given rights cannot be enslaved.

Much of the Western "Christian" world has become secularized in recent generations. One primary reason this has occurred is that Christians have lost a biblical worldview, and hence have acted, or failed to act, accordingly. Their ignorance of the truth has shifted the general direction of Western culture, from the path of liberty, justice, and prosperity (the fruit of the gospel) to tyranny, oppression, and lack (the fruit of humanism and secularism). Many nations are just beginning down this path and don't recognize the end result of basing a nation on secular ideas.

A biblical worldview and a providential view of history (at least to some degree) predominated in the thinking of the western world for most of the last thousand years. Those who led the western world usually had some aspect of a biblical worldview, including the non-Christians, while today a secular or humanistic worldview predominates, even among many Christians. Education has played a key role in this secularization. Christian education is how biblical truth is passed on to our children and others.

A Christian Philosophy, Methodology, and Curriculum

"Christian" means "that which pertains to Christ." As all aspects of education must pertain to Christ for education to be Christian, the following must pertain to Christ in Christian education:

1) Philosophy —why (also who, when, where),
2) Methodology — how,
3) Curriculum — what.

Many "Christian" schools and churches have humanistic philosophy, methodology, and/or curriculum.

What is Education?

Colossians 2:8 tells us that a worldly philosophy brings captivity: *See to it that no one takes you captive through philosophy and empty deception, according to the tradition of men, according to the elementary principles of the world, rather than according to Christ.* A worldly, humanistic philosophy in the present educational system of many nations has produced bondage within individuals' lives.

While a worldly philosophy brings captivity, the Bible tells us that a Christian philosophy brings liberty. In order to liberate a nation, individuals must be liberated first. True education is the primary means of imparting a Christian philosophy of life, and hence in bringing liberty to our nation.

In order to properly educate ourselves, we must first understand what true education is. Education does involve imparting information, but according to the Bible this is of secondary concern. Education includes instruction and discipline which is intended to:

[1.] enlighten the understanding,
[2.] correct the temper,

[3.] form the manners and habits of youth, and
[4.] fit them for usefulness in their future stations.

Education deals primarily with the inward man—with forming character. The formation of character is inevitable. Bad character, not good, is the result of the failure of public schools to discipline and provide moral education. Not only is the forming of good character neglected, but schools (including colleges) fail in the majority of areas of study to fit students for usefulness in their future stations. Many individuals lack creativity and entrepreneurship, because most of their educational experience was as a consumer of knowledge. True education must build producers — those who are able to take the knowledge they have and apply it to many new areas without someone always telling them step by step what to do.

The root of the word "education" has a dual meaning of "to pour in" and "to draw out." Both teaching (pouring in) and learning (drawing out) are involved in true education. Not only should we pour information and knowledge into a child, but we must make sure that they understand and know how to practically apply that which is taught. Education has not occurred until the students start producing.

Discovering a Biblical Method of Education

Having seen what biblical education is and agreeing that it is important, we must now ask: "How should we educate? Is there a Christian method of education?" To answer that question, we must first understand that methods are not neutral. Paul instructed the church at Corinth to be careful how they built upon the foundation he laid for the church (1 Cor. 3:10), for he understood that how you build something is just as important as what you build.

The content of the material taught in public schools is thoroughly humanistic and quite destructive of the godly character and thought in our youth (which in turn is destructive of our religious and political freedom and happiness). Not only is the content humanistic (and thus, destructive), but the method employed to teach these ideas is also humanistic and probably just as destructive as the content.

Using a biblical method to teach our children is essential if we desire to achieve our intended results. David and Israel of old learned the hard way that how you do something is just as important as what you desire to do. During David's reign as king, he had a good idea: "Let us bring back the ark of our God to us, for we did not seek it in the days of Saul" (1 Chron.13:3). Twenty years earlier, the Philistines had captured the ark of God during a battle with Israel. Now David desired to bring the ark into the holy city of Jerusalem. This was an excellent idea, but how he went about it proved of the utmost importance. Uzza would definitely testify to that truth, if we could talk to him today. As the ark was being transported from Abinadab's house on a cart, it was almost upset. Yet Uzza came to the rescue and reached out his hand to steady the ark. But this was the last thing Uzza did, for God struck him down and he died. David sought out the truth from God's word and discovered that using a cart to transport the ark was not God's way to move it, but the Philistine's way (1 Chron.15). He learned that **there is a danger in trying to do what is right in the wrong way.** In educating our children, we must seek to not only build what God wants, but to do it in the way he wants.

Being a Christian does not necessarily make one a Christian teacher. Not only must the reasons and motives for teaching (the philosophy) and the content of what is taught (the curriculum) be of Christ, but the method of teaching must be Christian as well in order for a truly Christian education to be provided. Taking humanistic methods or curricula and throwing in a few scriptures and a prayer does not make for instruction Christian. A sign on the school door or a chapel hour before class does not make what happens in the classroom actually Christian.

The Principle Approach to Education

If methods are not neutral and there is a Christian method of education, then what is that method? It is what has been called the Principle Approach. Briefly stated, the Principle Approach to education inculcates in individuals the ability to reason from the Bible to every aspect of life. As Christians, we know we are supposed to do this, but do we? Do we really know how to reason from the Bible to geography, astronomy, mathematics, or history, not to mention national defense, foreign policy, or civil government?

The Principle Approach restores the art of biblical reasoning.

We must again realize that as Christians we have the potential to be the greatest thinkers in all the world. Historically, Christians have been the leaders in almost every area of life (e.g. Johann S. Bach in music, Isaac Newton in science, Rembrandt in art, Adam Smith in economics, John Locke in civil government). To bring freedom, justice, advancement, and prosperity to nations today will require men who know how to reason biblically to all areas of life.

Most of the activities that are sweeping many nations today teach people not to think. Billions of dollars are spent on video games each year, with billions more spent on movies, sports, and other games. Amusement, which is derived from "a" and "muse," meaning "not thinking," is an apt description of these activities.

For example, television is used as a method of communicating information to our youth (and to ourselves). It takes little discernment to recognize that the content of most television programs is ungodly. Violence, immorality, anti-traditional values, and blatant and subtle humanistic ideas dominate the airwaves. As bad as the content is, the method is probably worse. What does a child do as he sits for hours every day in front of the television? The answer is nothing! His imagination, creativity and faculties of reasoning are not developed through the passive medium of television. Study after study has revealed that the more television a child watches, the poorer he does academically.

We are in great need today of restoring the art of biblical reasoning to our educational system. We may have more facts taught in our schools today (even though in many fields, major facts are conspicuously missing), but we must teach more than just facts. We must teach how to arrive at those facts as well.

To more fully understand the Principle Approach, let's look at each of the words separately. A "principle," according to a dictionary, is:

"1) The cause, source, or origin of anything; that from which a thing proceeds;
2) Element; constituent part."

A principle is like an element in chemistry. An element is the lowest form in which matter can exist naturally—it can be broken down no further. A principle is an absolute truth (and hence, biblical) that is reduced to its most basic form. While the Bible contains thousands of truths, these can be broken down into a small number of principles from which the truths spring forth. If these principles are known, this provides complete parameters through which to view
life, assuring that one truth is not forgotten while embracing a new one.

A "principle" and a "seed" are very similar in their meanings. A seed, being a plant in embryo, contains the entire plant - the whole thing is there, albeit in a condensed form. After a seed is planted, given some time, water, sunlight, and care, a huge tree can be produced. Likewise, principles are first given in seed form to children, yet these principles contain the potential of giant trees of truth and application. God starts with a seed and produces a plant.

The Principle Approach teaches seed principles over and over again in each subject and grade level with different illustrations, examples, assignments, educational methods, etc. This ensures that a child not only knows biblical principles, but that he lives them — that they are a part of his life.

Taking a few scriptures and forming an opinion on a subject is not sufficient. We must reason from the totality of the Bible, not violating any principle while seemingly adhering to the truth based on a few scriptures. If our conclusion on any issue violates any principle, then we can know it is wrong. Yet conversely, if our conclusion agrees with the foundational principles, then we can with humility assume that, although we still have more to learn, it is likely that our view is correct.

A Wholistic Method

The Principle Approach is also a wholistic method of education, that is, it is instruction from the whole to the part. We will use history as an example. Instead of teaching fragments of history throughout the various grade levels with seemingly no unifying factor among the different classes, a biblical approach would look at the whole of history first and then look at the parts in more detail, and those always in relation to the whole.

The whole of history can be looked at from a biblical philosophy because there is an overall purpose in history which unifies all the specific events of history. From a humanistic viewpoint, there is no purpose in history, and hence, no unifying theme which ties events of history together. This overall view and purpose of history is taught to a child from the very beginning of his schooling. He is given the overall picture to begin with, and then as he advances, the parts can be looked at in more detail. He will have an overall framework in which to put all the information he learns. Not only are the events of history centered around God and His Son Jesus, but the origin, development, and purpose of all fields of knowledge are directly related to God's plan in the earth. As this is understood, there will be a reference in which all information logically fits; hence, learning will not just involve memorizing a number of facts.

A truly biblical approach to education involves much more than just taking various academic subjects and trying to squeeze the Bible into them. A biblical principled approach to education will reveal that the source, origin, and purpose of all knowledge revolves around God and His plan for man.

How Do We Implant Principles?

If we desire to have a Principle Approach education, we must restore four key aspects of teaching and learning:

1) RESEARCH [study]: We must research the subjects and topics of interest from the Bible and other resources to identify basic principles.

2) REASON [think]: As we are researching a subject, we must continually ask ourselves what is God's perspective and purpose for the subject and what does this information reveal to me of God and His purpose.

3) RELATE [apply]: As we are researching and reasoning, we must also relate the truths uncovered to our own lives or to the situation at hand.

4) RECORD [express conclusions]: The principles and truths uncovered and related must be recorded or written down to accurately and permanently preserve them.

This four step process is the best way to implant truth within our hearts—the best method by which to learn and be educated. In most schools (and certainly most churches) today, students are seldom required to research, reason, relate or record in their pursuit of being educated. This is true in the everyday study of subjects as well as the tests on the subjects. Most tests are fill-in-the-blank, matching, or True-False. Students can take and pass these test for years and years without truly learning how to reason and think and be prepared for life after completion of school. Consequently, far too many people today do not know how to reason and think.

Practical Ways to Implement the 4 steps in the Educational Process

1) Essays

Writing essays is an excellent way to implant within the student the ability to research, reason, relate, and record. Writing essays enables students to truly express themselves—to communicate what they really know and believe. As one writes his ideas in complete sentences, he is forced to reason and think for himself. This personal expression brings liberty to the individual. He will not be dependent upon the media, teachers, or anyone else for his ideas, for he will have learned how to search out the truth for himself.

2) Notebooks

The compilation of notebooks by students on various subjects and topics is an excellent means of inculcating truth within them. Instead of being handed a textbook at the beginning of the year and memorizing pages of facts and information, in order to receive good grades, the student develops his own textbook by taking notes from the teacher and doing his own research and writing from various resources (which can include a textbook).

The notebook method not only assures that the student acquires knowledge, but it also builds character within the individual (which is the primary purpose of education). Self-government, industry, orderliness, discipline, and the ability to communicate and reason are only a few of the character qualities produced by the notebook method of education.

There are many other practical educational methods that can be used to make that the student actually is learning. Some include:
1) Verbal reports and tests
2) Complete sentences answers to classroom and test questions
3) Practical outlets for expression of all that is learned
4) Apprenticeship programs
5) Doing useful projects within the various classes

You can begin to see that a principle approach to education requires much work. While true education will be exciting and challenging, and not boring (one reason for the many discipline problems in schools today is that students are extremely bored), it will also require severe effort. If you have not exercised in many years and then participate in strenuous activity,
your body will hurt. Likewise, if you haven't exercised your mind for years and begin to use it strenuously, it will also hurt. But the more you use your mind, the better in shape you will be to think. Your mind is more than just a computer. It is like a womb, for you can get more out of your mind than you put in it. This is part of true reasoning.

Essentials for Christian Education

These elements are essential for an education to be truly Christian:

1) Teacher—A teacher who is a living textbook (2 Cor. 3:3) is the most important aspect of education. When you teach, you impart more of who you are than what you know. Students will read you. Therefore, to be most effective as a teacher, you must master what you teach so that it is a living part of you.

2) **Content**—In the material we teach, the Bible must be our central text (as we have discussed, not in a superficial way). While the Bible doesn't contain all the facts on all the subjects, it does contain all the principles and reveals God's purpose for each subject.
3) **Method** — In addition to a godly teacher and content, the educational method must also be Christian. This method should build godly character, impart a love of learning, and prepare individuals for leadership.
4) **Student** — We must view the object of our instruction from a biblical perspective; the student is a moral being created in God's image, yet sinful and in need of transformation and education in truth.

Biblical Scholarship is the ability to reason from Biblical principles and relate it to all of life. Not only did early Christians reason from the Bible, but even non-Christians were influenced by Christian schools in this manner and held to a Biblical worldview. This is quite the opposite of today for both non-Christians and even many Christians who now view life from a man-centered, humanistic worldview.

A world view is simply the way you look at the world around you. It includes your beliefs not just about religion but about family, civil government, art, music, history, morality, education, business, economics and all other areas of life. A world view is the set of presuppositions—that which is believed beforehand—which underlies all of our decisions and actions. These presuppositions determine our patterns of thought, which in turn influence our behavior. Our world view may be conscious or unconscious, but it determines our destiny and the destiny of the society we live in. It was the biblical worldview and scholarship of historic Christianity that provided the basis of a free and prosperous western civilization.

Higher Education

Historic Christianity developed a tradition of Biblical scholarship and established the best schools in every nation where they planted the church. But they also understood the need to train leaders at a high level. This is what led to their creation of the idea of the University in world history.

The first universities grow out of the church and monastic educational systems in Europe. They developed a curricula for not only the training of clergy, but for every key area of influence in a nation. So colleges or departments of law, medicine, business, mathematics, communication and political science emerged in the middle ages. All departments were rooted in the same source of truth – the bible. Leaders who emerged from such training felt just as holy a calling in the field of law or business as the clergyman studying theology. This produced leadership in western nations that gave much of the greatest achievements of science in the modern world.

Christians have to reclaim this mission and become leaders again of this historic universities, or start brand new ones that will eventually surpass the older ones. This is starting to happen with new institutions such as Handong University in South Korea and so many other places that are beginning to impact their nations by producing great leaders for good.

Chapter 9

Arts, Media, Entertainment

The Bible and the Arts and Media and Press

There are of course no references in the Bible to the means of communication that are available today such as television, motion pictures, radio, stereo, or newspapers. But the Bible does address the subject of the media in terms of the means of communication at the time. By studying this we can deduce certain principles that apply to any form communication may take.

The Bible speaks of communication in the form of oral history, drawings, sculpture, drama, dance, poetry, prose, music, writing on scrolls and parchments, parables and stories, preaching, etc.

The Bible shows the people of God using all of these forms of communication at various times. It also shows pagans using some of these forms for their own ungodly purposes.

We cannot deduce from the Scriptures whether each form of communication began by God inspiring one of His people to invent it or whether some pagan originated it. Historically we know that sculpture, drama, and music have been used since the most primitive of times. Ancient Egypt developed the use of elaborate pictures (Hieroglyphics) as early as 3300 B.C. and China did so around 1800 B.C. The alphabet was developed by the Semites and Phoenicians around 1600 B.C. The Egyptians developed papyrus for writing on around 1000 B.C and just prior to the Christian era they developed parchments. Paper was invented by T'sai Lun in China around 100 B.C., yet it was not used in Europe until around 800 A.D.

Although pagans invented many of the forms of media in ancient history, the Hebrews and Christians always had the approach that those things were in themselves but tools that could be used for good or for evil—there was nothing inherently wrong with any form of communication. Christianity for most of its history has always taken things of this world that were not manifestly sinful and stripped them of their pagan associations and ennobled them with godly content.

Christians up until this last century had an orientation toward life that said all things were spiritual and sacred. The idea of secular or worldly things was unheard of until the 20th century. Christians saw themselves as called to be involved in all aspects of the world as salt and light, not as some counter-culture group that needed to keep itself separate from those things that weren't specifically religious or church related.

For this reason, the people of God have historically excelled in the arts and other forms of communication. The poetry and prose of the Bible is unequalled. The musical culture of the Hebrews starting with David was prolific. The dramatic sermons of the prophets, which were acted out using many props, were very effective at catching the attention of the masses and conveying an important message. Hall and Wood write in *The Book of Life* of this effective use of the media by the prophets:

> *The prophets themselves used dramatic representations to enforce their great messages. Jeremiah went to the potter and got an earthen bottle. Then he called the elders of the people together in the valley of Hinnom. Holding the bottle in his hand, he preached a short and very effective sermon on the sins of the city. Then he threw the bottle down and broke it into fragments. After he had broken it, he said, "Thus saith the Lord of Hosts, 'Even so will I break the people and the city as one breaketh a potter's vessel, which cannot be made whole again.'" This was a most telling dramatization of Jeremiah's sermon. When the elders went home and thought it over, they would see that bottle broken in fragments and the remembrance of it would help them to remember the words of the preacher. . . . The prophet Ezekiel made a little model of Jerusalem in clay. Then he added the camp with the forts and mounds and battering rams of a besieging army. Then he took an iron pan and placed it between himself and the city. This was a dramatization of the way in which the city would be sieged. . . . The Passover was a vivid*

> *dramatic representation of the escape from bondage, enacted with great impressiveness in every home down to the present day. Part of the significance of the Lord's Supper lies in its dramatic representation of the sacrificial love of Jesus for his disciples, a memorial of his death "until he comes."*

Prior to the development of writing, the oral story of the Gospel was preserved by star-pictures (i.e. the constellations of the Zodiac) so that the ancient Patriarchs could enhance their communication by pointing up at the stars. These constellations are mentioned in the earliest book of the Bible, Job. God used the stars to communicate His promises to Abraham. It was these constellations that guided the three Magi (astronomers) to the city of Bethlehem to find the Messiah.

Jesus was a master at story-telling and the use of parables in order to communicate important truth to the masses. The Apostle Paul not only preached the Gospel orally as did other Apostles but also made use of "parchments" (2 Tim. 4:13) available at that time as a means of communication.

The Media and Arts in the Christian Era

The Christians put great value on communication via letters and written Gospels and preserved them over the early centuries of Christianity. Hall and Wood write of some of the contributions Christianity made in the advancement of various arts:

> *When the age of martyrdom was over and Christianity began to build its own churches, often upon the ruins of pagan temples, a new form of art came into being. The people were still ignorant and unlettered. How better could Bible stories be taught to the people than by picturing them upon the walls of the places of worship? These early pictures were of mosaic. They are called "Byzantine" because they originated in Byzantium, the old Constantinople.... After this period Europe was overrun by the barbarians of the North, and almost everything which was precious and beautiful was destroyed. Then came the forming of the great monastic establishments, and Christian art was saved by the monks, who*

themselves practiced, and taught the people, not only the practical arts — agriculture, metal-working, building; — but also the fine arts and crafts. However much monastic life may have degenerated later, the world owes to the monks of this period all its possessions of knowledge, saved from the utter wreck of the barbarian invasion. "Pictures are the books of the ignorant," said Augustine. It was necessary to teach the Bible to people who had no books, who could not have read them if they had had them. So the Bible stories began to appear again upon the walls of the churches in pictures and sculpture, crude at first but gradually growing more beautiful. . . . Then came the great building age all over Europe, lasting for nearly four hundred years, when the wonderful Gothic cathedrals were built, — such glorious buildings as those of Amiens, Chartres, Rheims, in France; Lincoln and Durham in England; Burgos in Spain. It was a time of great religious fervor. Everywhere over Europe churches were built, not only the great cathedrals but churches in every town and village. . . . The cathedral of Chartres . . . and its adornments (the windows and sculptures) tell the Bible history in stone. . . . These great buildings were built and the Bible was illustrated so completely in the carvings of the great western portals that Ruskin called that of Amiens, "The Bible of Amiens." Every important incident of Bible history is portrayed. . . . While these sculptures are crude, still they are very vigorous and expressive, and there was no more effective way of teaching the Bible to the people of that time. . . . In Italy there began to be felt the need of a finer way of teaching the Bible than by sculpture, and out of this desire came the development of pictorial art. The earliest period, which is called "The Gothic period," was from about 1250 to 1400. Among the earliest painters were Cimabue and Giotto. The paintings were upon the walls of churches in fresco, and the subjects were practically all

Biblical. . . . "Then came the periods of the early Renaissance, 1400-1500, and the later Renaissance, 1500-1600. To these periods belong the mighty masters; Raphael, Leonardo da Vinci, Correggio, Michael Angelo. . . . It must be borne in mind that this great development of art, the greatest the world has ever seen, was called out by the Church and was devoted to the church in its efforts to teach the Bible to the people. Many of these paintings are in galleries now, but originally they were painted for the walls and altars of churches."

The Canon of Scripture was completed in the first few centuries A.D. and by medieval times monasteries were organized and devoted to the meticulous copying of the Scriptures by hand on paper. While the Bible was being preserved it was largely hidden from the common man. Ignorance of the Truth resulted in a stagnant period in history, known as the Dark Ages, with little advancement in most areas of life. History shows that the introduction of the Bible in a society results in the advancement of all fields of life, including the arts, music, and communication. When John Wycliffe translated the Bible into the common English of 1382, he was providing the seed for the great change and advancement that would take place in every area of life in the following centuries.

In 1455 it is estimated there were 50,000 books total worldwide. In that year Johann Guttenberg invented the printing press in Germany. Ten years later the total number of books had increased to 10 million. It is easy to see why the printing press was a major breakthrough in communication. Due to the importance of its content, the first book printed on the press was the Bible. The distribution of the Bible to the masses caused Europe to arise out of the "dark ages", and was the reason the arts began to flourish as never before in such fields as paintings, sculpture, classical music, poetry, and prose. While non-Christians were involved in such media, by far most of the greatest contributors to the arts were Christians who felt called of God to glorify Him through that avenue.

The Dutch school of Art produced men like Rembrandt — the foremost painter of Bible subjects. Leader of the Protestant

121

Reformation, Martin Luther, took a popular tavern song and turned it into one of today's best loved Church hymns — "A Mighty Fortress Is Our God." English clergyman, Isaac Watts, compiled a hymnal that was used widely for many years. In the beginning of the 18th century two of the greatest classical composers of all time, Johann Sebastian Bach of Germany, the master of church music, and George Frederick Handel, famous for composing the "Messiah," set the early example of using Scriptural themes for their music. Charles Wesley and the Methodists contributed greatly to the communication of truth through the medium of hymns.

The first newspaper in the world was started in China around 1000 A.D.; the first in Europe was begun in 1615 in Germany and known as the "Frankfurter Zeitung." America's first newspaper was "Public Occurrences" established in 1690 in Boston. However, the main source of news in America for over 200 years came from the clergy through regular sermons on Sunday, as well as special weekday "political" sermons or lectures. This has been replaced today by the television news anchorman. News now is reported from a pagan worldview rather than a Biblical one. This is the greatest need today for new Christian leadership – to be owners and editors of the newsmedia.

How the Bible in the Hand of the Individual Produced Freedom of the Press

When the prophet Nathan confronted King David he gave an excellent example of the role of journalism—it plays a prophetic role in society, exposing darkness and reminding rulers that they cannot trample on the commandments of God. Likewise in the Roman Empire the idea that earthly thrones and authorities are subject to God's rule was a foreign concept to the world at that time, yet within a few centuries this truth had conquered the known world. The seed of the gospel continued to leaven Europe as Christ's message spread.

When the Bible finally became available to the common man, more and more courageous prophets spoke out and challenged the established political and religious systems of the day. John Foxe who is credited with being the first English-language journalist because he pointed his finger at the sins of the Catholic Church and recorded the abuses of popes and priests in his Foxe's Book of Martyrs—the first example of eyewitness reporting.

England was stubbornly resistant to the con[trol]
of the press. The British Crown suppressed all publ[ications on]
the principle that this would secure peace and publi[c order. The]
Christian poet John Milton, however, made an early [case for]
freedom of the press in his famous Aereopagitica, p[ublished in 1644.]
He summarized a truly Christian idea when he wrot[e, "Let her and]
[truth] and falsehood grapple; who ever knew truth put to the worse,
in a free and open encounter?" This idea was penned centuries
earlier by the author of Proverbs, who described Truth and
Falsehood as competing in the open market of ideas.

Should the highest officer of any government on earth
flagrantly abuse the authority of his station, or by adopting public
measures hostile to the public good, it is not a crime, but the duty of
a free people to speak evil of him. The tongue in this case is the
proper weapon, where the laws of men cannot reach.

Counter-Cultural Christianity

With the explosion of so many new forms of communication
in the 20th century, Christianity should have the easiest time of any
period in history to be the salt and light of the world. This means not
just evangelism and communicating about "religious" subjects, but
influencing the entire culture in every sphere of life by educating in a
Biblical worldview.

Unfortunately, the 20th century has instead proven to be the greatest
period of apostasy and secularization of American culture.

Pagan philosophy has become dominant in the television,
radio, music and movie industry. And the sad thing is that this has
not happened because paganism conquered Christian thought. Rather
it has happened simply because Christians began to accept a faulty
theological premise in the late 1800s that taught them to separate
from the things that were "worldly" or non-spiritual and that it was
useless anyway to waste your time in such things because things
were going to get worse and worse before the end-time return of
Christ. Thus, although it happened very slowly, by the 1960's
virtually every influence of Christianity on the media had
disappeared and pagan worldviews and philosophies were allowed to
gain the ascendancy by default. Now Christians see themselves
largely as an irrelevant counter-culture and thus the world sees them
that way as well.

From 1933 to 1966, Christians in America influenced ..nunication flowing from Hollywood. Scripts were read by presentatives of the Roman Catholic Church, the Southern Baptist Church and by the Protestant Film Office. During that period, there was no sex, violence, profanity, or blasphemy in movies. For the most part, movies and television programs communicated the true, the good and the beautiful. Hollywood studios and producers once followed the Motion Picture Code, which stated:

> 1) No film or episode may ridicule any religious faith.
> 2) Ministers of religion should not be portrayed as comic characters or as villains.
> 3) Religious ceremonies should be carefully and respectfully handled.

But in the 1960s, Christians abandoned its role and Hollywood put in its own ratings systems that have now proved virtually irrelevant at preventing the "f-word", taking the Lord's name in vain, vulgar references to excretion, intercourse or the genitals, implied or actual sexual intercourse, explicit nudity, moderate or severe violence, depictions of alcohol and/or other drug abuse, etc.

Now there are new reviewers. Christians have been replaced as script reviewers by homosexuals, feminists and Marxists. These groups award pictures and television programs which communicate their point of view and make sure contrary views never receive any Academy Awards or other recognition.

A Strategy for Reformation of the Media

Christians have been diligent to claim every new form of media communication for evangelistic purposes and have done quite well at it. But most Christian programming takes place rarely in prime-time; most is found in the "religious" time slots on Sunday mornings. Few have worked to invest their time into using media to communicate in a comprehensive way. Few Christians have worked at going into the major newspapers and magazines and television networks and Hollywood with the goal of bringing a Biblical worldview to bear upon it. If Christians have gone into these fields it's been largely for personal career reasons—very few having a goal beyond perhaps witnessing for Christ to their associates. There have been successful films with Christian themes (for example, *Chariots of Fire*), yet these are often not been the product of the Christian community.

The same is true of music, drama and dance. The Christians have their "religious" music, etc. which witnesses for Christ but few are infiltrating or buying out the mainstream companies for such art. In the world of painting and sculpture, Christians are constantly complaining about the filth that is funded by the government and displayed in public art museums. Christians with a solid Biblical worldview need to become the directors of such museums and government agencies, but when have you last heard of a teenager in one of your evangelical or charismatic churches talk of such a career? Such things are too worldly for them or just unimportant compared to religious goals.

In addition to making films and starting newspapers that are designed largely for Christians, we must also provide resources in the arts and media that will impact all men with a Biblical worldview. As Augustine might say today: "Television, movies, and videos are the books of the ignorant." Christians must utilize this source of the arts to communicate a comprehensive view of life that is Christian to the hundreds of millions of ignorant men in the world today.

Christian businessmen need to be investing and buying out the major television networks and motion picture studios and theatre chains across the country. They need to be buying out the major newspapers. They need to be buying out the major music studios and record companies. They need to reestablish a Hollywood film office and motion picture code that is godly. Good News Communications led by Ted Baehr is working to do this and provide movie reviews based on a truly biblical worldview, in place of Hollywood's broken ratings system. It is important that we are there being a watchdog of what trash pagans produce, but why should we expect them to produce anything else?

Christians need to go beyond that and become the producers themselves and not just the reviewers. The idea of spending so much money on such things seems to be hard to rationalize, especially when Christian media-ministers tell you that you should spend it instead on funding their shows. But until we once again see that this is true spirituality and that it is essential for redeeming our culture, it will never happen. We will still go on as perhaps a significant number of the population, yet complaining in our living rooms that our side, the pro-life, pro-family, pro-morality majority never gets fair coverage in the news or decent programs on prime-time. The media will continue to control the elections, the public opinion, the framing of the debates of the issues of our day. It is time for those who are Christian to establish themselves in the arts and for the Christian community to back them. The arts and media must become central in the church's protest against the pagan world.

Jesus and the prophets were the master story-tellers of their time. The media is simply a story-telling tool. We need to imitate our Lord and once again take up the weapons of our warfare which are "mighty in God for pulling down strongholds, casting down arguments and every high thing that exalts itself against the knowledge of God, bringing every thought into captivity to the obedience of Christ" (2 Cor. 10:3-5).

The development of communications technology radio, television, telephones, internet and satellite systems are a great opportunity for the church, especially where there is freedom of religion, speech, and the press. Christian journalist Lee Grady writes:

> These tools have now made even the most tyrannical nations vulnerable to the principles of the gospel and made them accountable to public scrutiny....And everywhere the seed is planted, the Christian idea of man and government takes root. It happened in America. It is happening today in Moscow and Bucharest and Prague. It will most assuredly happen in Beijing and Baghdad and Teheran.

Chapter 10

Business

Right in the garden at the very beginning He gave man "work" to do (Gen 2:15). This was the foundation of the institution of business and the marketplace. The word **"business" or "bank"** is not found in the chapters where the duty to work was first given by God, but that is the institution that was being created by God's own design. Man's labor resulted in fruit or a product that was then saved in some location or was able to be traded for other things. This is how the idea of a market developed. So business is a divine institution that all people are a part of. Even if an individual does not formally have a job, he still interacts with the marketplace by buying, selling and trading with those who do. It is worth noting that in the greatest commandment Jesus also said we should love our neighbor ". . . as [you love] yourself" (Lk. 10:27). Self-preservation is the driving force behind the calling of work – to provide for the survival of ourselves and our loved ones.

This command was given to all humans on earth, not just to Christians or people of faith. They were human responsibilities and are essential best-practices that must be modeled rightly by Christians for the world to work as the Creator intended for our good.

A Christian Economy and Factors of Production

Economics is the science that deals with production, distribution, and consumption of goods and services. Christian Economics is the discipline that studies the application of Biblical principles or laws to these characteristics. Biblical economics details how men are to use God-given natural resources, ideas, and energy to meet human needs while glorifying Him.

Christianity produces internal liberty in man, the foundation for a Christian economy. The internal change of

heart that Christ gives should produce Christian character and the self-government necessary for economic prosperity. Christian character and self-government in a nation produce people who:
- do not steal. Billions of dollars are lost each year by businesses to employees. This theft is much greater than stealing by non-employees.
- have a strong work ethic.
- will save and invest to acquire greater return later.
- are concerned for their posterity and pass on a greater estate than received.

The truth of the gospel brings new ideas and creativity to man, thus increasing his material welfare because he can create new and better tools. In addition, man gains the understanding that God has given abundantly. When man seeks His supply, he will find it.

The introduction of Christianity will also manifest itself externally in political freedom, the result of internal liberty. A government the acts on Biblical principles is a prerequisite for a Christian economy. The economy lives in the government's "house." Its policies must promote and protect economic freedom.

Economic liberty flows from a combination of personal and governmental freedom. This freedom includes owning property, choosing an occupation, keeping the fruits of labor, and trading in a free market. Economic freedom is evident when wages and prices are determined by voluntary exchanges of free men and women and not by the government.

Man's material welfare is a product of natural resources combined with human energy and coupled with the use of tools. Christian economist Charles Wolfe represents this concept by the following formula:

$$N.R. + H.E. \times T. = M.M.W.$$
Natural Resources + Human Energy x Tools = Man's Material Welfare

If *Natural Resources* increase, so does *Man's Material Welfare*. If *Human Energy* is exerted, *Man's Material*

Welfare increases. If better tools are created, *Man's Material Welfare* will also increase. This equation for *Man's Material Welfare* is applicable for every nation in the world. However, there is a vast difference in those who have a biblical worldview and who apply their physical and mental energies than those having a secular perspective.

In a Christian Society with Great Economic Freedom:

Natural Resources

God created man with certain basic needs, such as food, clothing, and shelter. God created everything needed to meet those needs. God created natural resources. Men with a biblical worldview believe that God has provided everything necessary and therefore men have faith to seek, find, and process abundant natural resources. As the Natural Resources available to man increase, his material welfare increases as well.

Human Energy

God not only created natural resources, but He also created man with ~~human~~ energy. God told him to "have dominion" or rule over the earth (Genesis 1:26). Man was placed in the garden to cultivate and keep it (Genesis 2:15), which required labor. After the fall, cultivating the ground required additional "sweat" (Gen. 3:19).

In a Christian society, men are inspired by God to work. In a nation of economic freedom, men partake of the fruit of their labors, encouraging the exertion of more energy. As man works harder and exerts more human energy, his material welfare (and that of the nation) increases.

Tools

Man was unable to cultivate the ground, rule over the earth, or even meet his basic needs well with his bare hands alone. To take the natural resources God had created and produce food, clothing, and shelter, tools were needed to till the soil, cut down trees and saw timber, mine and refine minerals, and tend sheep and weave wool. Knowing this, God gave man ideas for inventing and making tools. Man was given intelligence and physical strength, mental and muscular energy, to take the natural resources and create tools.

Man has always used tools. Adam and Cain were farmers and likely used simple tools to plant and cultivate, and cutting tools to harvest grain. Abel was a shepherd and likely had a rod and staff.

Hammers, axes, plows drawn by oxen, millstones for grinding meal, furnaces for refining silver and gold, ovens, and baking and frying pans are tools mentioned in the Bible. A tool's usefulness is measured by the amount of time and energy saved and the increase in the quantity and/or quality of the goods and services that can be produced through its use.

The following chart reveals how advancements in agricultural tools have produced economic progress (tools are a multiplying factor in the equation of man's material welfare):

Time period	Tool	Production by one man
Adam	Simple tools	Food for Eve & himself
Abraham	Plow and Oxen	Food for large family
18th Century	Iron plow and Horse	Food for 3 families
1940's	Tractor	Food for 14 families
Today	Advanced Tractors	Food for 60 families

Improved tool development has always occurred in nations where people have access to the truth of the Bible and the mind of Christ. Rodney Stark effectively shows this in the book *The Victory of Reason: How Christianity Led to Freedom, Capitalism, and Western Success.*

Advancement in tool development causes man's material welfare to improve. Man's productivity is a result of better tools and better uses of those implements. We must be diligent in our work. God has given man all he needs for his human welfare—natural resources, human energy, and ideas for creating tools. Using labor, man transforms God-given resources into the food, clothing, shelter, and other things that meet his human needs. Labor is the title deed to property.

In a Secular (or erroneous religious) Society with Limited Economic Freedom:

When a non-Christian worldview or secular society considers the equation (Natural Resources + Human Energy x

Tools = Man's Material Welfare), the perspective is quite different from a Christian worldview.

Natural Resources

A secular society lacks faith in God's providence and, consequently, men find fewer natural resources. The secularist or socialist views the world through limited resource glasses, believing the world is like a pie needing to be divided so that everyone gets a slice. In contrast, the Christian with a correct biblical worldview knows his potential in God is unlimited and there are no shortages of resources in God's earth. The resources are waiting to be tapped.

This world is not deprived or limited in resources. Known reserves of minerals and energy resources are greater today than the mid-twentieth century despite increasing consumption. Ideas allowing us to tap into unused natural resources are limitless. Native Americans wiped oil on their faces 100 years ago. Today, new uses of petroleum have transformed our economy and brought a higher standard of living for everyone. In recent years, the computer world has been revolutionized by the silicon chip, which is made from the same component in sand.

While many secularists view the world as over-populated, Christians know that God has made the earth sufficiently large, with plenty of resources to accommodate all the people He knew would come into existence. There is room and food for the entire world population today. Five billion people on the earth could live in the state of Texas in single family homes with front and back yards and be fed by production in the rest of the United States. Present world agricultural areas, if developed by present technology, could feed 31 billion people. See Max Singer, *Passage to a Human World* to study this further. Economist Thomas Sowell also addresses this in his writings. Our earth has plenty of room and natural resources.

Human Energy

Those with a secular worldview lack God-inspired strength and work ethic. Such strength and character creates more production hard labor, honesty, investment in the future, etc. In addition, secular nations with limited economic freedom cause men to exert less energy since they cannot eat of the fruit of their labor. The net result is that man's material welfare suffers.

Tools

Secularists are cut off from the Bible and the mind of Christ (the chief source of creativity) and get fewer ideas for inventing new and better tools. Lack of new or improved tools keeps production and man's material welfare from increasing. A good discussion of this historically is found in a book by Rodney Stark entitled *The Victory of Reason: How Christianity Led to Freedom, Capitalism, and Western Success*.

Comparing the factors of production in Christian and secular societies reveals why some countries prosper and some do not. While men and women in every country try to multiply their human energies with the help of tools in order to transform natural resources into useful goods and services, Christian free societies are more efficiently than others.

A study of incomes of different nations and people groups confirms this observation. Protestant countries had higher per capita income than the catholic countries. But non-Christian countries have low incomes or rampant starvation.

In a Christian economy people earn more with less work meaning:
- People will have more free time for worship of God, instruction, recreation, and service to others.
- People will have more money to give to Churches, charities, and foreign missionary efforts.
- People can acquire more luxuries.

Real wealth of a nation is determined by the number of hours worked needed to buy a certain commodity compared to the same statistic in another country.

N.R. + H.E. x T. = M.M.W., applies to every country in the world. Societies built on Christian principles will have a proper view of natural resources, the character to exert human energy, and access to the creativity of God leading to better tools and increased production. While any nation adhering to this truth will see the material welfare of its citizens increase, most people and nations are quite poor. In fact, 46% of the world lives in poverty today. Why? Some claim that it is because many nations lack natural resources. Yet, some nations, such as Japan, with few natural resources are quite prosperous, while there are also many nations with abundant natural resources that are much less prosperous.

The primary reasons that nations are in poverty is lack of spiritual resources and truth. A secularist worldview that limits production will stifle man's material welfare. False religious concepts in the culture of a nation can hinder economic success. The economic state of a nation depends upon its religion.

The Wheel of Progress in a Christian Economy

Man's material welfare increases in a Christian society because Christian faith and character help enlarge, vitalize, and improve production. But the economic incentives of freedom are also important. To find and process natural resources such as oil and minerals is extremely costly. So is the protracted process of researching, developing, and producing new and more efficient power tools. The profit motive provides individuals with the needed incentive in a Christian free economy based on individual enterprise.

History shows that in a Christian free economy men invent more and better tools, invest more in producing those tools, and use those tools more efficiently than in a secular society with limited economic freedom. Socialistic and Communistic economic principles eliminate the profit motive and cause people to be less productive. Taking away private property does not make people happy or cause them to flourish, as many ancients, such as Plato, or modern men, such as Karl Marx, have espoused.

The individual parts of a productive economy are illustrated by a wheel with a hub, an outward rim, and spokes.

The Hub of God-Given Liberty

A Christian Economy revolves around man's heart where Christ brings internal liberty. This God-given liberty that begins internally and is manifested externally becomes the hub of the wheel of progress in a Christian economy.

It is important to recognize this liberty is granted by God and not by man or the state. If the hub of the wheel is seen as freedom granted by man or the state, rather than by God Himself, then that freedom can be taken away. A continuing, consistent free economy cannot exist if freedoms can be removed.

The hub, seen as man's internal God-given liberty, has a reliable core to which the various spokes—the Biblical principles of economics—can be securely attached. Only the hub of God-given liberty can give rise to the various spokes, for it is the economy of liberty where men are allowed to practice individual enterprise, economic self-government, and manifest each aspect of the spokes.

The Rim of Stewardship and Law

In a Christian economy, the spokes in the wheel of progress are held together, and the wheel runs smoothly when the discipline of God's law and the practice of Christian stewardship are exercised. The interplay of God and man determine the rim of responsibility that maintains economic freedom under God's control.

The great challenge to maintaining freedom is preserving order. To accomplish this, people must be disciplined from within so they do not infringe upon the rights of others. When men understand and obey God's law for a Christian economy the following happens:
- Men respect each other's property. Unfortunately, people need locks on their cars, walls, and fences. Guards protect houses and business to keep others from stealing property. Growth of the economy is hindered greatly in this environment.
- They do not cheat one another. For a nation's economy to grow, the people must be honest.

- They abide by contracts.
- When citizens are elected or appointed to positions in government, they do not use their power to secretly erode the value of the people's money through inflation, nor do they restrict the people's economic freedom through excessive regulation. A Christian businessman in a developing country needs raw materials to quickly pass through customs so that large orders for various customers can be filled. Before these materials are released, forty-six signatures from government officials are needed with most wanting a bribe before a signature. When the extortion is refused, materials are delayed, orders are not filled on time, and credibility and finances are lost. Excessive regulation and dishonesty stifle economic growth.

To maintain economic freedom, individuals practice Christian stewardship by being:
- industrious in earning money
- disciplined in saving money
- wise in investing money
- obedient by sharing God's law with their church and with those in need
- Frugal and restraining urges to buy items that are advertised to bring instant gratification
- Self-sustaining and not needing government for assistance.

The Spokes of the Economic Wheel:
1. Individual Enterprise and Giving

God's Principle of Individuality expresses that every person on earth is distinct, unique, and important to the economy and therefore has:
- special God-given talents as a producer that leads to specialization and division of labor (producing greater wealth in a nation).
- individual desires as a customer.

- individual rights, such as entering an occupation of personal choice (promoting -greater productivity), starting a business, and buying the goods one prefers.
- individual economic responsibilities to provide for self, family, and the poor rather than rely upon the civil government to meet needs.

Providing for the poor is the responsibility of individuals, families, communities, and the church. When the state assumes this responsibility, the church and individuals will eventually believe that government should take care of the poor.

Welfare states are not biblical and do not work. Many nations in recent decades prove this point. While government money spent on welfare has increased dramatically, so has the nation's poverty. The vast majority of every dollar allocated for the poor and needy is consumed by the governmental bureaucracy which has no intention of fixing a problem. Government money is not the solution to poverty.

The Bible says that the family and church are the primary institutions of health, education, and welfare. When these responsibilities are reclaimed, the civil government can eliminate spending hundreds of billions of dollars on welfare. Individual enterprise opposes economic collectivism and its emphasis upon the group, and applies the Bible Principle, "as you sow, so shall you also reap," which encourages productivity.

2. Economic Self-Government (Free Enterprise)

An individual who governs himself will direct and control his own economic affairs in a responsible manner. He will be a self- governed:

- producer— not needing constant supervision to assure the quality and quantity of his work.
- customer— buying only the necessities and never exceeding income through spending. John Locke says that the measure of property is not how much one wants, but how much one needs— what is sufficient for an individual to fulfill God's will in his life.

- saver— regularly saving some of his earnings to assure a strong economic future.
- manufacturer or retailer— producing and selling quality goods and services, with due concern for the rights and needs of employees and customers.

A nation of self-governed people will grow the economy and keep it free.

3. Christian Character (Honest Enterprise)

Christian character is the foundation for a free and prosperous society. A few specific character qualities that affect the economy of a nation include:

- Diligence and industry — hard work increases productivity and increased prosperity.
- Faith in God's Providence— hard work alone does not guarantee prosperity; there must be trust and obedience in the Lord to experience His blessings (Matt. 6:33; Deut. 28). Individuals and nations must put faith in God to experience His blessings.
- Love for our neighbor — as we express Christian love, we will care for the needy in the land.
- Honesty — employees will not steal from their employers; an honest civil government will not steal from its citizens by use of fiat money (money not supported by a tangible asset such as gold or silver).

4. Private Property (Private Enterprise)

The Principle of Property teaches that property is first, internal and property rights are necessary for a free and prosperous society. Other freedoms (religion, speech, etc.) when compared with a general distribution of real property among every class of people are relatively less significant for maintaining freedom. If people have property, they have power. This power can be exerted to prevent a restriction of the press, the abolition of trial by jury, or the abridgement of any other privilege.

5. Local Business (Local Enterprise)

Economic growth occurs as small businesses are started locally by responsible individuals who are prepared. They do not depend on others for employment, but save money, develop an idea that benefits or serves others, start a business, becomes self-employed, win customers, and then employ others. New jobs are now created and the economy grows.

Christian education produces knowledgeable and motivated individuals when these concepts are taught. Biblical worldview Christians do not expect government to create jobs. They expect entrepreneurs to assume responsibility for themselves and others.

6. Voluntary Union (Free Market)

A voluntary working together of all peoples and regions of a nation will encourage economic growth and prohibit tariff barriers while creating a nationwide "common market." Each person in each region or district would create his/her best by using the local natural resources, exchanging the goods and services for the production of others, and using honest money as the medium of exchange. Each person is free to sell or not to sell at whatever price, never forcing anyone to buy. Exchange of goods and services is voluntary and occurs when all involved benefit from the exchange.

The price of goods and services is determined by "supply and demand." In a free market, the supply of goods and services will balance out the demand for those goods and services at a price that buyers are willing to buy and sellers are willing to sell. The greater the supply of any particular kind of good or service will mean a lower price. The greater the demand for any kind of good or service will create a higher price.

The Road Bed: A Christian Constitutional Form of Government

A civil government built on biblical principles provides the road on which the wheel of economic progress can turn with greatest efficiency. Such a government, rooted in the Law, the Gospel, and based on the Christian idea of man and government, assists economic progress by providing an environment of orderly freedom. Production and exchange flourish, private property is protected, theft and fraud are punished, and economic needs are not provided by the government. Such a government will be limited in action and expenses with just enough power to guard personal freedoms but not enough to hinder honest economic activities.

Even if a business leader is a strong Christian with great character and a solid worldview regarding business practices, an understanding of the government's oversight of business operations is important. Government is similar a house. If the house is well built, the owner is able to live more healthy than in an unhealthy environment where problems can arise. The same is true of economies. The economy lives in the house that government built. It affects the economic health of everyone. It is not enough to have good business people. The government must establish the proper framework .

Christians Needed in Banking

Much work needs to be done to bring godly economic reform to the nations. One of key areas is in the banking and finance industry. Corruption will never diminish unless we get better leaders. This is an important area for Christians to take the lead.

Becoming knowledgeable of the principles of Christian economics is the beginning place of this reform. The next step is to instruct the citizens and leaders of a nation and then to begin to act upon these principles. The result will be a gradual increasing prosperity for the entire nation.

Chapter 11

Health, Medicine & Science

A Biblical View of Health and Healing Process

In Deut 7:15 and Exodus 15:26 God told His people that if they followed His law "...the LORD will take away from you all sickness, and will afflict you with none of the terrible diseases of Egypt which you have known; ....I am the Lord who heals you." God provides a supernatural protection but gives instruction in living. The natural result is good health. In the New Testament Jesus made healing of people's bodies a primary part of His mission and told his disciples to "go and do likewise." Furthermore Matthew 8:17b says that through His death "He Himself took our infirmities and bore our sicknesses."

God created man distinct from the animals. He gave man a soul and spirit (non physical) and a body (physical). Both affect the presence or absence of health (Genesis 1:2628; 2:7). Being created by God gives to all humans worth (Genesis 1:27) regardless of the quality of life or usefulness to society.

Perfect health is a Biblical concept that has been experienced only by Adam and Eve prior to their sin (Genesis 2:17b; Romans 5:12; 1 Corinthians 15:21,22). Optimal (not perfect) health since the fall is best achieved through spiritual regeneration, Biblical obedience, and current medical knowledge. Medical wisdom must always remain within the framework of biblical authority (Nehemiah 8:10b; Psalm 90:10; 2 Corinthians 5:17; Exodus 15:26; 1 Kings 3:14; Psalm 38; Proverbs 3:7,8; 2 timothy 3:16,17). Optimal health is never be achieved through medical knowledge alone (Exodus 15:26; 1 Kings 3:14; Psalm 38; Proverbs 3:7,8).

Healing may occur through the body's natural processes, God's supernatural act, or demonic forces, concurrent with or entirely separate from standard medical intervention (Matthew 7:21-23; Luke 10:34; 1 Thessalonians 2:9,10; 1 Timothy 5:23; James 5:14-16). Miraculous healing is always possible and was never limited to any particular time of history (James 5:14-16). God allows some Christians to experience acute and chronic disease, disability, or deformity (Job 2:4-8; John 9:1-3; Hebrews 12:5-11; 1 Peter 1:6,7). The absence of healing is not necessarily due to a personal sin or a lack of prayer, faith, or spiritual maturity (2 Corinthians 12:8,9; Philippians 2:27; 1 Timothy 5:23). Spiritual regeneration and biblical obedience are absolutely essential to a biblical concept of mental health (Ephesians 4:9-16; 2 Timothy 1:7; James 1:6-8). Psychiatrists should promote mental health through evangelism and a thorough application of Biblical principles for their patients (Nehemiah 8:10b; Psalm 90:10; 1 Corinthians 15:1-19; 2 Corinthians 5:17).

The ultimate cause of all disease, deformity, disability, and death is the sin of Adam and Eve (Genesis 2:17b; Romans 5:12; 1 Corinthians 15:21,22). Complete understanding of these conditions is impossible on a purely natural or physical basis (Genesis 2:17b; Romans 5:12; 1 Corinthians 15:21,22). Medical problems are frequently caused by personal sins (Proverbs 23:1921,29-34; 1 Corinthians 3:17; 1 Corinthians 6:9,10). However, the presence of disease, deformity, and disability does not necessarily imply God's temporal judgment on the person afflicted (Job 2:4-8; John 9:1-3; Acts 3:2).

In the Garden of Eden, Satan got an opening to attack through what Adam and Even consumed. Satan used food to entice. He used food to tempt Jesus. Before Jesus was betrayed and was crucified, He gave His disciples the means of grace known as holy communion using food as a way to remember His sufferings. Food symbolizes spiritual warfare, both our failure and our redemption through Christ's victory.

Diet is actually directly linked with health (much could be said about diet but is beyond the limited scope of this chapter).

Much of the Old Testament discusses nutrition, hygiene, sanitation, and diet. God told His people to wash with running water and separate from others when they had a discharge, i.e. a runny nose, an oozing infection, etc. Today we know that these discharges are filled with germs.

Another source of sickness is sin, and forgiveness of sin and healing are linked as well (Luke 5:23-24). But Jesus stated that because a person is sick, one cannot assume that it is because of sin (John 9:2-3). Although God sends disease as judgement on the enemies of His people, it does not follow that He gives His people sickness to teach them something.

Exodus 15 said God promised He would be their healer. Psalm 103:2-3 says He is the one "who heals all your diseases." We will always encounter disease in this fallen world. There is no promise from scripture that we will never get sick while on this earth. We are not promised perfect health, but we are promised healing. Total health is more than just the absence of disease.

Medicine and Health Care were historically a Christian idea

In the Hebrew Republic the priests were the medical practitioners/doctors. It was a part of the ministry calling of God. Likewise, Christians have been prominently involved in health care throughout history. Luke, one of the authors of the Gospels, was also a physician (Col 4:14). In 100AD, one of the earliest church documents outside of the Scriptures was the *Didache*. It taught believers: "Thou shalt not...commit infanticide (nor) kill a child by abortion." Abortion was widespread in the culture of the Roman Empire at the time.

A church leader named Tertullian in 200AD said that all the churches had a common fund to support widows, disabled, orphans, and the sick. The Council of Nicaea in 325AD instructed churches in major cities to start a hospice, to providing medical care and shelter for the poor.

The most famous person in the early history of medicine was Basil of Caesarea in 369. This Christian minister started the first hospital called a xenodochia. The term "hospital" was not used however until the 12th century. Basil's 300 bed hospital cared for the seriously ill, disabled, and victims of the plague. Basil and later Chrysostom also started orphanages.

A few years later Paula was one of the first nurses recorded in history. In c390 the third hospital in history was founded in Rome (first in the west) by Fabiola, a wealthy widow who became a nurse. In 650, nuns took took care of the sick at the Hotel Dieu in Paris. Charlemagne of France decreed that every cathedral should have a hospital attached in 800AD.

Later many Protestant missionaries were doctors or took doctors with them. Dorothea Dix fought for the humane treatment of the mentally ill worldwide in the 1800s. In 1860 Florence Nightingale started her work as a nurse. In 1864 Jean Henri Dunant & four others formed the Int'l Red Cross.

The priestly calling to heal, reconcile and relieve the distressed

Health care and medicine were practiced by God's people. God gave the Israelite priests responsibilities for dealing with disease in their nation. God's laws provide instructions on sanitation so that good health was possible in the community.

Doctors and medicine were never condemned by God but were condemned as idolatry if people sought human doctors and medicines without seeking God Himself (Jeremiah 46:11b). Galatians 5:19-21 declares that the abuse of drugs is witchcraft. The Greek word for witchcraft is pharmakeia. The English word pharmacy is a derivative. Medicines or drugs that provide altered states of mind deceive the body into a delusion that there is nothing causing pain, when in fact there is. A regular habitual use of drugs to alter our state of mind is sinful and actually occultic. It is proper to use medicine at times but if not also searching for the CAUSE of the disease then problems arise.

Medicine is biblical. Ezekiel 47:12 refers to the use of trees, leaves, oils, incense, and plants for medicine. These are alternatives to other drugs and surgery. Even if a certain medical practice works it does not mean it is approved by God. Abortion works but is immoral and criminal by God's standards. If a common traditional medicine is accepted in a community, the believer is still responsible to evaluate it biblically and ethically.

The "art of the apothecary" is mentioned in Exodus 30:25. Oils were used for ceremonial rites and healing the sick as well. In Numbers 16:46-50 Moses told the priest Aaron to use incense to stop a plague. We know that incense and oils are highly anti-infectious and anti-viral and God uses natural things for supernatural results. In the New Testament Jesus told the story of the good Samaritan and said the would of the man were treated with oil.

A biblical approach to medicine allows the body to heal itself, treats the person as a whole, deals with the cause rather than the effect, and views prevention as the best cure. These elements should not be confused with so-called "natural" methods that may have occultic associations such as homeopathy, meditation and yoga. A believer must be informed and learn to discern the differences.

The Calling of Medicine and the Need for Worldview Training

The health care worker must have a thorough knowledge of the Bible practically applied to his personal and professional life (2 Timothy 3:16,17; 2 Peter 3:1). The Bible is the final authority for health, medical care, and medical ethics (2 Timothy 3:16; 2 Peter 3:1). The Bible does not conflict with medical science when both are correctly understood (Genesis 1:1-2:25; Colossians 2:3). Medical ethics should not be determined by the desires of the patient, the ethics of a medical organization, current medical practice, technical feasibility, or governmental legislation (2 Timothy 3:16,17; 2

Pet. 3:1). Medical ethics must be determined by the truth found in God's Word.

The health care worker has a priestly calling because health involves the whole person (Luke 4:18; Hebrews 12:13; 1 Peter 2:9). Medicine and the Church are related fields of service (1 Corinthians 6:1-8; James 5:14-16). Christians should have other Christians for their physicians (when they are available) because medicine is a priestly calling (1 Corinthians 6:1-8; James 5:14-16). Both priest and doctor have the goal of saving people, one of the body and one of the soul.

Fundamentally, health is not a product that can be purchased from healers but rather the result of a way of life that doctors as "teachers" help us to know. When believers hear a priestly calling into medical practice (Matt 11:5) it becomes foremost a sacred vocation with a non-economic motive. A person with this calling makes the best doctor. It does not deny them profit, for the laborer is worthy of his wages (1 Tim 5:17-18), but it creates a better doctor who serves. When medicine is filled with people who lack this calling they easily slip from the healing calling to the use of medicine to kill (i.e. abortion, euthanasia, etc). Today, killers are accepted in the profession as equal partners and undermines the respect for the calling.

The pagan term "physician" meaning a healer was replaced in the Christian era by the term "doctor" meaning teacher. This is because of a biblical worldview that turns the focus from trusting in the power of the human doctor to the power of God's word that, if understood and followed by the patient, will bring healing.

Training of health care workers and practice of medicine in the pagan secular world today virtually ignore the spiritual side of man, the reality of God and revelation, and the historical role of the healer as a priest. This situation reflects the dominant view of Western society that man is only an evolved animal or bio-chemical entity. In this pagan view medical ethics are relative and offer no concrete answers to the complex dilemmas of today's advanced bio-technology.

At the same time godless secular Man believes that he is the master of his own fate and can "improve" his physical and mental abilities through drugs, artificial reproduction, and genetic engineering. This idolatry of human ability in medicine is itself one of the causes for health care costs to continuing to rise above the resources of individuals and society. The doctor must regularly rest and worship on one day in seven (Exodus 20:8-11), and medical care cannot habitually supersede the Sabbath without consequences (Exodus 20:8-11).

Responsibility and Economics

The pagan idolatry of the physician has been revived in modern culture and has also led to liability lawsuits because of blame placed on the practitioner for the inability to produce perfect health. Christian doctors and patients take a more humble approach. There is no such thing as total liability. Men can do their best and no more. Pagan patients expect a doctor to work miracles (actually magic) and tolerate no failures. This is an impossible burden on medical practice and leads to unlimited malpractice suits, leading to risk-aversion and referral of patients to others. But risk is basic to medical innovation and the saving of lives.

Christians cannot expect a guarantee of healing or health from a human being. Health cannot be purchased like a commodity. Humans are finite, limited, and differ in experience and competence. Therefore one cannot assume a guarantee of knowledge or skill nor criminal intent or negligence. Trust of a doctor is godly but idolatry (or hostility if expectations not met) is not.

Not only is the pagan idea of total liability wrong, so is the concept of limited liability. A person who causes harm through negligence is biblically responsible to make restitution. Limited liability leads to society's responsibility for restitution. Responsibility is wrongly shifted from the individual to the environment and the community. Someone or something else is to blame for imperfection.

The idea of national health insurance and socialized medicine are based on these faulty pagan concepts and leads to unrealistic "equal" distribution of resources, the growth of the state, and the loss of freedom and prosperity in any society that adopts it. When health is called a human "right" it actually starts to empower the state, rather than the individual, and thus reduces individual liberty. Furthermore, it is an illusion to think something becomes less costly when the state takes it over. Only criminal malpractice falls within the state's jurisdiction. But there is no basis for state licensing or regulation of medical practice itself. State control cannot eliminate imperfections or bad motives.

Licensing of medical practice was not done for most of the past two thousand years of Christianity. It is only common now in the neo-pagan resurgence. The only solution is for the Christian faith to shape people with strong moral character who will enter the medical field as a calling. The state cannot make moral doctors nor can the law bring salvation. Socialized medicine is no more workable than the Constitutional prohibition of alcoholic drinks. State controls never limits profit, only quality.

The Role of the Individual and the Family

God expects all to be responsible for their own health by following His ways. The primary responsibility for health maintenance, disease prevention, and medical care belongs to the family, as it is defined Biblically (Genesis 2:24; Exodus

20:12,14; Ephesians 5:22-6:4). No other institution may assume this primary responsibility, especially over minor children except in an emergency that is clearly life-threatening, without the consent of one or both parents (Genesis 2:24; Exodus 20:12,14; Ephesians 5:22-6:4). I Timothy 5:8 says that it is the family that is responsible for care of the family's health and well-being, not the government.

Paul speaks about the role of the family in health with he says in 1 Timothy 5:10 that a wife should be "well reported for good works: if she has ...washed the saints' feet, if she has relieved the afflicted..." All believers are exhorted in Romans 12:13 to be "...given to hospitality." Likewise 1 Peter 4:9 said Christians were to "be hospitable to one another..."

Hospitality was especially required of bishops (1 Tim 3:2). Early Christians understood this was not just having people over for dinner. It meant caring for the physical needs of others who were hurting and sick. Early Christian bishops therefore led the way in the emergence of hospitals, etc. Ezek 34:1,4 warned "the shepherds of Israel, [that]....The weak you have not strengthened, nor have you healed those who were sick, nor bound up the broken...." This certainly had a spiritual meaning but included the physical needs as well. God holds shepherds of His people responsible for healing the sick.

God gives the family and the church responsibility to care for the sick. There is nothing in Scripture that gives this role to the state to provide health care; only to ensure safety. The state has no jurisdictional role that allows it to violate the privileged communication between a doctor and his patient. The confession between a priest and parishioner is answerable to God alone.

The health care worker should receive payment for his services as determined by the free market (Matthew 10:10b; Luke 10:7; 2 Thessalonians 3:10; 1 Timothy 4:18b), but being a priestly calling, the primary motivation of the health care worker should not be financial gain (Titus 1:7; 1 Peter 5:2).

Issues at the Beginning and End of Life

Individual human life begins with the fertilization of the human egg with the human sperm (Genesis 4:1; Numbers 11:12; Psalm 51:5) and the embryo conceived by this process must not meet any other criteria to attain the full ethical and legal status of a person (Psalm 51:5; Matthew 18:8-10). Induced abortion is murder except to save the physical life of the mother (with medical advancements, that option is extremely limited if not eliminated) and participation at any level is sin (Exodus 20:13; 23:22-25; Psalm 51:5; 139:13-15; Jeremiah 1:5). The choice of the mother must never take precedence over the life of the unborn child, and detection of abnormalities or defects in the unborn child is never grounds for induced abortion (Exodus 20:13; Psalm 139: 13-15).

Likewise, infanticide (the killing of a child after birth), either by deliberate action or by inaction, is murder (Exodus 20:13). Intervention with an unborn child at any stage after conception should be permitted only to correct clearly defined physical disease or deformity when sufficient evidence exists that the potential benefit to the child clearly outweighs any harmful effects or the possibility of death (Psalm 139:13-16; 1 Corinthians 6:19,20). The unborn child should receive medical treatment that is no less careful or necessary than that provided to any human being (Genesis 4:1; Psalm 51:5).

Euthanasia (the killing of adults due to low quality of life), either by deliberate action or by inaction, is murder (Exodus 20:13), and intervention in the disease process of a terminally ill patient is an ethical course of action (2 Corinthians 5:1-9; Philippians 1:21). Only the patient's physician, in consultation with other health care workers, the patient, and the patient's family, is able to assess ethical treatment or non-treatment of the terminally ill (James 5:14-16), and living wills improperly hinder these decisions (James 4:13-17; 5:14-16).

All men and women will inevitably die (except Christians who are raptured at the Second Coming of Christ) because of the sin of Adam and Eve (Genesis 2:17b; 3:19b; 1 Thessalonians 4:17; Hebrews 9:27), but no one has the "right to die" by any means or for any reason, and so-called "death with dignity" is incompatible with a Biblical understanding of death and sin, (Exodus 20:13; Ecclesiastes 8:8; Romans 14:7,8; 1 Corinthians 6:19,20; 15:56). The exception is the honorable and loving choice for a man to lay down his life in voluntary sacrifice for another (John 15:13).

The image of God in all patients and the love that Jesus Christ calls us to give to all people, determines the quality of care and comfort of the terminally ill (Genesis 1:26,27; Matthew 25:32-46). Water, food, and air should never be withheld from patients, nor has anyone the right to refuse these basics of life, when their medical conditions allow these substances to be taken by natural routes (Exodus 20:13; Matthew 25:32-46; 1 Corinthians 6:19,20). Suicide is a violation of the Sixth Commandment (Exodus 20:13) and never a Biblical solution to any life situation (John 10:10; 1 Corinthians 10:13; Philippians 4:19).

Genetic Engineering, Transplantation; & Drugs and Drug Abuse

Alterations of human genes before or after birth should be strictly limited to the correction of clearly defined disease or deformity when sufficient evidence exists that the potential benefit to the person clearly outweighs any harmful effects or the possibility of death (Genesis 4:1; Psalm 51:5). Man does not have the wisdom to change human genes except to correct clearly defined physical disease or deformity (Psalm 139:13-16; Luke 4:40; James 5:14-16).

Fertilization of the wife's egg by her husband's sperm is the Biblical pattern of reproduction (Genesis 2:24; Matthew

19:4-6), and fertilization of the egg of a woman with the sperm of a man who is not her husband is not Biblical (Genesis 17:19-21; 38:24). The Biblical location for conception and development of an embryo or fetus is its biological mother (Deuteronomy 6:4-9; Ephesians 6:4), and the conception and development of an embryo and fetus should not take place within any in vivo or in vitro location other than its biological mother except possibly for the few hours needed for in vitro fertilization and the growth of the embryo(s) to the stage that allow for its (their) transfer (Deuteronomy 6:4-9; Ephesians 6:4).

Transplantation of human organs is ethical and does not violate the sanctity of the human body when Biblical standards govern the treatment of both donor and recipient through deliberate peer review (Matthew 19:12; John 9:1-3; Acts 3:1,2), but the premature pronouncement of a patient's death in order to obtain his donor organs is murder (Exodus 20:13; 1 Corinthians 13:3).

Drugs may be used under the proper supervision of health care workers in diagnosis and treatment (Luke 10:34; 1 Timothy 5:23; James 5:14b), but are not necessary or sufficient in the diagnosis and treatment of all medical conditions (Luke 12:22-34; John 4:32-34; Romans 14:17; 1 Timothy 4:7,8). Health care workers should work to prevent drug abuse and dependency with patients who require drugs that affect the mind or senses (Proverbs 20:1; 23:29-35; Ephesians 5:18; 1 Peter 4:4), and medical care should not be administered on the basis of chemical determinism as the only explanation of disordered states of the mind or senses (Genesis 1:26-28; 1 Sam 21:13-15).

Abuse of such substances as drugs and alcohol involves physical disease, spiritual bondage, and distorted personal relationships (Proverbs 23:29-35; Ephesians 5:18; Genesis 9:20-23; 19:30-38). Treatment of substance abuse cannot rightly exclude ministry to the whole person (Romans 12:3; Ephesians 5:18; 1 Timothy 1:7).

The Bible gives adequate guidance for the sphere of Medicine

This mountain or area of influence in culture is not left by God to humans to decide right and wrong for themselves. He has given principles and guidelines for its practice.

Christians led the way in creating the medical sciences for most of church history. Today it has been seriously eroded in the modern western world by a neo-pagan ethic. A new generation of medical professionals who understand their priestly calling and are willing to boldly stand up against the perversion of it is necessary.

Chapter 12

Government

Early in Genesis came another command – to "shed" the "blood" of murderers (Gen 9:6). This responsibility was the foundation of the institution of civil government. To punish crime in a fallen sinful world was given to man by a loving God for the protection of innocent human life. The word **"government" or "politics"** is not found in the chapters where the duty to punish murderers was first given by God, but that is the institution that was being created by God's own design. Even if an individual never directly is involved in making or upholding law and justice, nonetheless each person is born with certain rights and responsibilities of a citizen. In free democratic nations this means that electing good government leaders to do the job of punishing criminals and protecting innocent people is the duty of every citizen.

This command was given to all humans on earth, not just to Christians or people of faith. They were human responsibilities and are essential best-practices that must be modeled rightly by Christians for the world to work as the Creator intended for our good.

The father of the Constitution of the United States, James Madison, noted that democracies "had been spectacles of turbulence and contention . . . incompatible with personal security or the rights of property." Pure democracy, therefore, is to be avoided. How? By the concepts of representation and fixed higher law, which are associated with the term "republic."A
Biblical form of government may better be termed a representative democratic republic or a constitutional democracy. Henceforth, these elements should be kept in mind when we use the general term "democracy." To say "democratic republic" or "representative democracy" or "constitutional republic" would be better.

We need to define the practical aspects of democracy even further if we want to avoid the mistakes of other democracy movements of history. Following are seven basic governmental structures that are revealed or at least implied in the Bible and are necessary to protect and secure individual rights and liberties. These comprise the essential framework of a Godly government.

The Framework of a Constitutional Republic

Decentralization of Government—Federalism

The pagan tendency is always to centralize power. This began with the building of the tower of Babel in Genesis 11 which God condemned. Since power residing in the people is a basic premise of democratic government, government should be kept as close to the people as possible. This can be accomplished by establishing a small national government and strong local and regional governments.

The Hebrew Republic had a government that was a decentralized, family-based system. It had local town and tribal (regional) governments that were independent of the national government. They were known as the elders of the cities who met in the gates (Exod 24:1; Num 11:16,17).

Such a division of powers safeguards against the tyranny of centralization since it ~~will~~ allows the people to most fully participate in government and to keep watch over the flow of power through the governing officials. (For example, in 1 Kings 12:1-16, it seems that had Rehoboam listened to the people and his counselors, the nation of Israel may not have split.)

History has shown that centralization of governmental power destroys the liberty and the rights of man. The way to have good and safe government is to divide the power among the people and the localities, instead of entrusting it to one body. Civil government in a country should be subdivided into many levels (local, regional, national). The power of each level should be clearly defined and sovereign in those defined areas. No level of government should be able to usurp the jurisdiction of another. A great majority of the power should rest on the local level.

The limited powers of the national government should be clearly defined in a constitution and limited to those things which affect the country as a whole, such as defense, foreign policy, regulation of interregional and foreign commerce, citizenship laws, coining money, and copyrights. All other powers should remain with the people, or with the local, and regional governments. The powers of local and regional government can be written in a regional constitution and include such things as traffic regulations, business regulations, public works, voting procedures, law, and order.

Jesus Christ taught the principle of limited government and sphere sovereignty in Matthew 22:36-40. He said that "Caesar" may only do certain defined things, and that the other institutions, such as the church and the family, have their defined responsibilities and, therefore, sovereign rights of jurisdiction. This is true also between national and local governments.

Constitutionalism

The concept of constitutionalism began with the Hebrew Republic when Moses presented the Book of the Covenant to the people at Mount Sinai. It contained the Decalogue and the companion body of law. Contrary to impressions that one may have of this as being an arbitrary top-down imposition of law, the reality is that, although the laws were written by God, they were read and submitted to the people for adoption. In Exodus 19:7 Moses came down from Sinai with God's law for the nation but instead of imposing it upon them it says that he "called for the elders of the people, and laid before them all these words which the Lord commanded them." In other words, he submitted to them for their evaluation and adoption or not.

The good news was that in verse 8 "the people answered together and said, 'All that the Lord has spoken [regarding the nation's law] we will do.' So Moses brought back the words of the people to the Lord." We do not know how long this deliberative process took place, but the elders had taken to their tribes and received a conclusion from the citizens of the nation and brought that news back to Moses. It is important to note that the omniscient God of Israel did not really need for Moses to tell him what the people had decided, but the text is there to make an important point for us to understand – that no government is just that is not based on the consent of the governed.

This consent in Israel was not emotional and immediate. It was a lengthy and informed process. This is evident for the first consent of the people saying "we will" was not sufficient for God to implement the new system. It took two more readings of the law and deliberation by the people and their vote in the affirmative before it became binding upon them. This is explained in Exodus 24:3-6. "All the people answered with one voice and said, 'All the words which the Lord has said [i.e. the national covenant] we will do.'....Then he took the Book of the Covenant and read in the hearing of the people. And they said, 'All that the Lord has said we will do, and be obedient.'" It was only after a second consent by the people that it was recorded in a permanent written form called the "Book of the Covenant" and then the people of the whole nation were finally all assembled to hear it a third time read by Moses himself to them. At that final consent, it then became their binding constitution.

Later Israel's king entered into a covenant with the people where he promised to govern according to the Book of the Law, which was their constitution (1 Chron. 11:3; Deut. 17:14-20). For David, it mattered not that he was already anointed by a prophet of the Lord; he had to enter into a covenant with the people's representatives as well. This biblical idea that "just powers are derived from the consent of the governed" is expressed in the United States Declaration of Independence which says that "just powers are derived from the consent of the governed."

Federalism comes from the Latin word "Foedus" meaning covenant. A written constitution or contract will enable the people to see if the national government oversteps its authority. This usurpation of power can be resisted by the local and regional governments rallying together. In a decentralized republican form of government, a constitution, and not the national ruling party, is supreme and should only be amended with the consent of the people.

A government of liberty will be a government of laws, not of rulers or the majority. In a pure democracy, a simple majority (just over 50%) holds power. The rights of the minority could be in jeopardy under such a government. Therefore, a constitutional democracy makes the law supreme, and protects the rights of all people.

Throughout history, people have been governed by laws imposed by their rulers where citizens had no voice. In a democracy the people form their own constitution and consent to it. Hence, they establish a government of people's law, not of ruler's law. Both the people and the rulers are subject to the law. This is essential for protecting the individual's rights to life, liberty, and property. Citizens must not only be protected from harmful acts of other citizens, but also from abuses by their own government. Since the law is supreme and not the rulers, the people will be protected from a ruler's tyranny.

A constitution defines and limits the power of government. It acts as a chain to bind down rulers from misusing power. It is written so that it will not be forgotten. Any government gives freedom to its citizens, no matter what structure it has, when the laws rule, and the people are a party to those laws. Any government opposed to this will be one of tyranny.

A constitution formed by the people should not deny the rights of others. The laws will apply to all people equally, regardless of political position, religion, race, wealth, social status, or creed. Everyone is equal before the law in relation to protection of their life, liberty, and acquisition of property.

A parliamentary form of government is where the supreme source of law is the Parliament rather than a fixed higher written constitution. Parliament tends to favor whatever groups gain the majority coalition and potentially may oppress the rights of minorities and individuals as it pleases. Any approach to rights based on ethnic or special group rights is ultimately dangerous to the rights of those groups or individuals out of favor with the government in power.

Separation of Powers

A significant difficulty in forming any government is to first enable the government to control the governed and then insure that the government controls itself. Men tend to abuse power, especially if they are given too much. It has been said that all power tends to corrupt; absolute power corrupts absolutely. Therefore, power must be limited in our civil rulers.

We have seen that prescribing specific powers in a constitution is one way to accomplish this. Another is to separate governmental powers into different branches with different personnel overseeing each branch. Every government (whether a monarchy, oligarchy, democracy, etc.) exercises these three functions: legislative – lawmaking, executive – enforcing and carrying out laws, and judicial – interpreting laws. In the Hebrew Republic there was recognition of these three functions in Isaiah 33:22. It said that "The Lord is our King, the Lord is our Lawgiver, the Lord is our Judge." God being perfect and all wise can exercise all functions righteously, but sinful, finite men cannot.

There should be a division of functions and personnel between the legislative, executive, and judicial departments. It is necessary to set up three separate branches with prescribed separate functions (in a constitution), where no person may have power in any two branches at the same time. This serves as an internal control of abuse of governmental power. Since men are not angels and tend to lack consistent self-control, separation of powers will guard against tyranny.

The French political writer, Montesquieu, wrote in *The Spirit of Laws* (1748):

> *When the legislative and executive powers are united in the same person, or in the same body of magistrates, there can be no liberty; because apprehensions may arise, lest the same monarch or senate should enact tyrannical laws, to execute them in a tyrannical manner. Again, there is no liberty, if the*

judiciary power be not separated from the legislative and executive. Were it joined with the legislative, the life and liberty of the subject would be exposed to arbitrary control; for the judge would be then the legislator. Were it joined to the executive power, the judge might behave with violence and oppression.

Tyranny will result when legislative, executive, and judicial powers are all accumulated in the same hands, of one, a few, or many. This is also true of all rulers, whether hereditary, self-appointed, or even elected. Simply giving power to the people and allowing them to elect their leaders is not an assurance of securing liberty for all. One thousand despots would be as oppressive as one. Separating governmental
powers into three branches is one of many governmental controls needed to keep the people's rights and liberties from being endangered.

The three branches should be independent of each other with no one branch having total control of another. As an example, the legislative branch should not be able to remove the executive or judiciary very easily; and the executive should not be able to dissolve the legislative or judiciary. While independent, these branches should not be completely separate, but should band together through a system of checks and balances. This will permit each branch to guard against one department encroaching into another, which would result in tyranny.

An example of checks and balances is the executive having the right to veto laws passed by the legislature, and the legislature being able to override the veto with a larger percentage vote by their members. A well-defined system of checks and balances will help maintain the separation of powers in three branches. While a separation of powers will produce some conflict between the branches of government, this will assist in preserving the three branches of government and the system of checks and balances. To preserve them is as necessary as to institute them.

Independent Judiciary and Trial by Jury

Another check on sinful men abusing their governmental powers is having a court system with judges independent of the executive or legislative branch, and by having trials by jury. In a nation under law, any violation of the law requires a judge. Wrongdoers must be punished and required to make restitution to deter crime, yet, there must be an orderly process of justice where the guilty and innocent are distinguished. Judges should not only be knowledgeable of the law, but also honest, ~~refuse~~ refusing bribes, and not show favoritism.

The Hebrew Republic emphasized an independent and impartial judiciary (2 Chr 19:5-10; Exod 23:1-3; Deut 17:6; Lev 20). It also asserted in passages such as Deut 19:15-19 that (1) One is innocent until proven guilty, (2) there is a right to due process of law, (3) One cannot be forced to testify against oneself, (4) Accusers must be personally present to confront you so they may be cross-examined, and (5) the right to appeal to a higher court (Deut 1:19).

History is replete with examples of judges manipulated by government authorities to further their political agenda. An independent judiciary is essential to ensure that the written boundaries established by a constitution are maintained. The judicial system should be made up of un-elected individuals who will not be swayed by political pressures. The courts keep an eye on the legislative and executive branches of government and determine their faithfulness to constitutional standards.

Individual judges, even if un-elected, may at times be manipulated by other government leaders to render unjust decisions, against political opponents of the government. Therefore, in order to protect individual liberty, and guarantee a fair trial, a judicial system needs a jury drawn at random from society. These jury members should generally be on the same social level as the defendant. They also should be from the same city or geographical area as the defendant, yet should not know any facts about the case in advance that might bias their perspective. The jury must be protected against government reprisals in order to be independent. A jury of peers is effective because it relies on a plurality of people to judge of the defendant's character and the credibility of the witnesses.

There is freedom in a society that guarantees that life, liberty and property cannot be taken from the possessor until a dozen or so of his countrymen pass their sentence upon oath against him. Government becomes arbitrary without such a system of justice, allowing the legislature to pass oppressive laws or a judge to deliberately misinterpret the law.

The jury system was foreshadowed in the Hebrew Republic (Deut 19:15-21) and in the teaching of Jesus concerning taking cases to the people (Matt 18:15-17). It was fully developed in British law over 1000 years ago. Governments, whether fascist or communist, have forbidden trial by jury. The United States conducts about 120,000 jury trials each year.

Civilian Police and Militia

Another crucial curb on the power of sinful men in government is a civilian-dominated and controlled police and militia. The Hebrew Republic clearly separated the leadership of the army from the Executive branch; Moses was the Executive and Joshua was the Commander of the military; David was the king and Joab was the commander of the military. These commanders would have authority over a small peacetime professional army such as David had in his 600 man bodyguard and forces for use in emergencies until the militia could be gathered (1 Sam 23:13). These commanders would lead the overall military strategy of the militia when they were called out in times of war, but the militia divisions had their own locally elected officers (Deut 20:9; Num 31:14). The members of the militia supplied their own weapons which presupposed the right of any citizen own and use weapons (1 Sam 25:13; Num 31:3; 32:20). Any attempt to prohibit the right of an individual to own arms was unbiblical and is a pagan attempt to centralize power (Judges 5:8; 1 Sam 13:19-22). The leaders of the local militia could refuse to serve if they judged that a war was unjust (2 Sam 20:1; 1 Kgs 12:16).

Military and police power are a necessity in society to protect citizens from criminals and enemies, both foreign and domestic. A wise and prudent people will always have a watchful and jealous eye over this power. The supremacy of the civil over the military authority is an essential principal of free government.

World history has proven repeatedly that the "people's" armies are there to protect the people's interests as a whole, but are being used by powerful government leaders to further their goals. Many nations experience military coups regularly and the generals of the armies run the nation rather than "presidents" and "constitutions."

In order to ensure civilian control of the military, a constitution could establish an elected head of state ("president") as the commander-in-chief of the armed forces in war time. However, rules for the military should be established by elected representatives of the people other than the head of state. These elected representatives should not be able to spend money for armies for more than the period of time until they face re-election. This keeps the support of the military power by the representatives subject to the approval of the people.

The officers of the armies should not be appointed by the head-of-state, but by elected representatives from their own geographical area. The majority of a nation's army should simply be working citizens who have their own weapons and can be called together quickly. By doing this, no permanent army can exist that can be manipulated of by a political leader. This system allows any citizen to own his own weapon, which will give everyone the ability to defend himself, and will also give a geographic area of people the ability to defend themselves from armies that do become pawns of the government.

The police force should be locally and regionally controlled and completely separate from military power. The head of the police forces should be elected and governed by local government. The rest of the police should be hired by the government as normal employment.

Election of Representatives

Another crucial part of the framework of free government is the election of representatives. Although those governmental powers and offices are severely limited and checked, the men who are to fill those positions must be elected by the people and forced to face those same people frequently in order to be re-elected. This establishes accountability.

Half of the national legislature of the Hebrew Republic was composed of an elected house of officers called "judges" which were selected on the basis of population, not regional or tribal representation (Deut 1:13-17; Exod 18:21-26). Another house in their legislature was composed of two appointed "elders" and two scribes/lawyers representing each geographic region (tribe) plus the 24 priests totaling 70 men. This unelected body was known as the Sanhedrin.

The elected representatives of the people however were chosen on the basis of population: 10s, 50s, 100s, and 1000s. Moses would swear them in or "appoint" them only after they were selected by the people (Deut 1:13).

Frequent and free elections are essential meaning that those who run for office can do so without restriction of being from one party. One party may possibly dominate elections but it must come through winning the battle in the free marketplace of ideas. The right of any citizen to form a party and offer candidates for election is essential.

The vote in a nation must not be compulsory if it is to be free. It must be voluntary and available to all citizens equally, regardless of race, color, social status, religion, or gender. The vote must also be by secret ballot so that no pressure or fear of reprisal can influence the outcome.

Once the election determines the winner there, must be a commitment to the peaceful transition and relinquishing of power by the previous office-holders. It is essential also that all competing candidates and parties work to be unified for the common good of the nation.

It is crucial that not all government offices be filled by popular choice. In order to prevent the politicization of the judiciary, for example, it would be best that judges remain appointed by elected representatives. Another safety necessary to prevent majority tyranny and ensure more healthy gradual change in a nation would be for different portions of the legislative and executive branches, on both the national and regional levels, to be up for elections on different years. This would prevent radical changes from taking place without time for the electorate to fully weigh the potential consequences.

Independence of church, press, and schools

Jesus answered the question of his opponents in Matthew 22 regarding paying taxes to Caesar by saying to render "to Caesar [i.e. the government] the things that are Caesar's, and to God the things that are God's." (Matt. 22:17-21).

Before giving this answer Jesus asked for a coin and He held it up and asked His audience whose image was there. They answered that it was Caesar's image and then He gave His answer - give taxes to Caesar. But the second half of His answer was to give to God what belongs to God. The idea of the image conveyed a thought that Jewish hearers would understand but the Roman authorities would find innocuous. Caesar's image on the coin represented his rightful jurisdiction over tax issues, but in like manner God's image would represent an area of life that God alone had jurisdiction.

God's image is found in the man's soul and mind. It is something uniquely given to us by God and therefore we should never yield control of it to any human authority, especially the state. The practical outworking of Jesus' answer was revolutionary and contrary to the universal pagan idea of government that claimed jurisdiction over every sphere of life. The Jewish hearers understood Him to clearly express that whatever relates to mind, speech and worship, and related institutions should remain independent of government control. In other words, educational systems, media, the press, and all assemblies for communication and worship were subject to no earthly authority.

After centuries, this political teaching of Jesus Christ became the basis of the modern western idea of separation of church, media and speech from the powers of the state. It was a Christian lawyer in the United States named James Madison that put the concept into the U. S. Constitution in 1789 saying that the government can "make no law...prohibiting the free exercise [of religion]...or abridging the freedom of speech, or of the press..."

Family, Schools and Media are the three areas of life, other than Church itself, that operate in the sphere of the soul and mind. These are powerful in the shaping of culture and the future of a nation. These should be completely independent of the control of the state. Pagan governments claim the right to control them but biblically, they do not legitimately have such authority.

These seven structures of government, based upon biblical ideas and models, provide safeguards for the protection of individuals' God-given rights to life, liberty, and property. Remember that the purpose of civil government is to protect law abiding citizens and punish criminals. These structures are some of the ways that this protection is assured.

Though it is important to establish biblical structures of government, it is more important for the citizens of a nation to continually work to place godly men in office who can establish justice even without an ideal form of government. Although good laws do well, good men do better. We need both. In the next chapter we will discuss how to get good government leaders and keep them.

SECTION THREE

Chapter 13

The Five Signs of Transformation of a City or Nation

Teaching All That I Commanded

Christian nations that once had a strong biblical worldview and godly institutions repeated the folly of Israel. God warned of the danger of apostasy once they entered the promised land and began to enjoy prosperity and peace. A few centuries later, a generation arose in Israel that was unfaithful to the God and traditions of their fathers. This is true for many so-called Christian nations. They began to neglect the things that produced their freedom. They lost their virtue and self-government and became prey to internal dangers more dangerous than any external enemy. When people lose their virtue they will be ready to surrender their liberties. When biblical morality and worldview are strong among the citizens, they will never be enslaved.

"Tares" are sown when the church is "asleep" i.e. neglecting her role in society (Matthew 13:24 and Proverbs 24:30-34). If a nation's problems were the result of some conspiracy of men, the solution would be beyond the reach of most of us. Fatalism, apathy, and despair would be understandable. Since God says the real problem began with our neglect, then the solution is within our grasp. If we accept our responsibility and do our duty, we have grounds for hope.

When we correctly identify and diagnose the true cause of a nation's problems, we can solve them. Christians today are likely to place the blame on various conspiracies of men: the humanists, the ACLU, the big bankers, the Trilateral Commission, the New Age Movement, the World Council of Churches, the Homosexuals, the Feminists, the Communists, the Pope, the media, etc. Information regarding such groups and their activities can be useful, but must never be regarded as the source of our problems. God forbade it in Isaiah 8, verse 12 and 13: "You are not to say, 'It is a conspiracy!', in regard to all that this people call a conspiracy. And you are not to fear what they fear or be in dread of it. It is the Lord of hosts whom you should regard as holy. And He shall be your fear, and He shall be your dread."

Israel was facing judgment, destruction, and an end to their dreams. Many Christians today feel things are hopeless and fear these non-Christian groups more than they fear God. This attitude diminishes the true Biblical understanding that God is Sovereign over the earth. God sees human conspiracies and laughs at them for He knows what He has planned will prevail. This should be our perspective toward conspiracies. Psalm two says:

> "Why are the nations in an uproar, and the people devising a vain thing? The kings of the earth take their stand, and the rulers take counsel together against the Lord and against His Anointed: 'Let us tear their fetters apart, and cast away their cords from us!' He who sits in the heavens laughs; the Lord scoffs at them. Then He will speak to them in His anger and terrify them in His furry: 'But as for Me, I have installed My King upon Zion, My holy mountain.' I will surely tell of the decree of the Lord: He said to me, 'Thou art My Son, today I have begotten Thee. Ask of Me, and I will surely give the nations as Thine inheritance...' Now therefore, O kings, show discernment; take warning, O judges of the earth.... Do homage to the Son, lest He become angry, and you perish in the way..."

This prophecy describes the first coming of Christ, His death, His resurrection, and His absolute authority to reign. Prior to His ascension, Jesus delegated this responsibility and authority to His church saying, "All authority has been given to Me in heaven and on earth. Go therefore and make disciples of all nations."

In the great commission Jesus gave pastors the primary method of their work: education. They are not personally required to be involved in politics, media, schools, medicine, and reconciliation. However, their main task according to Ephesians 4:12 is to equip the saints for the work of the ministry. When a church's leadership faithfully is "teaching them all that I commanded," then transformation of a nation is possible.

Practically, a church must expand its Sunday sermons and discipleship programs beyond the exclusive focus of individual salvation, personal piety, and victory in life. Many churches include in the bible classes and small-group curriculum a focus on family. Some churches teach work and business. But church curriculum should include all of the six key areas of influence in culture - Family, Business, Education, Media, Health Care, and Government. A model of discipleship is illustrated below.

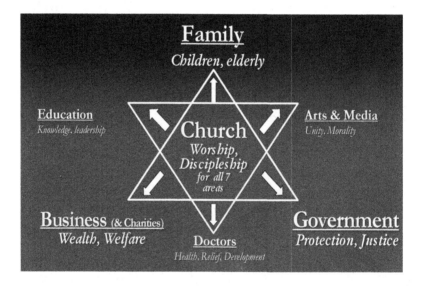

The church must train people in a biblical worldview. This is Christ's Great Commission vision – go and disciple all parts of every nation! Christians had great impact in different nations over the past two millennia. It can certainly happen again.

In the parallel passage of the Great Commission found in Mark 16 Jesus added "signs" that would follow this mission.

He detailed a way to measure progress of evangelism and discipling nations:
- "cast out demons"
- "speak with new tongues"
- "take up serpents"
- "drink anything deadly"
- "lay hands on the sick"

Most people see this in a personal manner, but Christ's reference to "nations" declares these signs should be equally applied to the larger mission as well. Churches have to re-evaluate their mission and measure themselves differently. Size of crowds and buildings are irrelevant. Jesus and the New Testament writers had no regard for such things. The relevant question is this: Are churches manifesting the "signs" Jesus mentioned in the Mark's version of the Great Commission? Are they producing people who effectively deal with demonic powers in the culture? Are members within a church healing the culture, communicating to the culture, and confronting the corrupt leadership of the culture? Jesus said these kinds of signs should be following our work.

In this book we have presented the historic biblical best practices of the church in history for discipling nations. Let us now summarize these:

"Casting Out the Nation's Demons"

There are three fundamental best practices to help Christians deal with cultural sin and spiritual oppression and help the community to "Cast Out its Demons":

- City-oriented Research-based Unified Prayer and prophetic Proclamation
- Apostolic outward-oriented and service-oriented strategic Evangelism and wholistic Revival
- Pastors providing Worldview Training and Mobilizing Christians in coordinated 7-Mountain strategy

Jesus told his followers to disciple the nations. He expected them to "cast out demons" from individuals and nations. Their mission was to become effective in deliverance from the national sins and spiritual oppression over society.

The church has been given authority to shape history. If our nation is in an awful condition, God holds us responsible. In 2 Chronicles 7:14 He says: "If... My people who are called by My name humble themselves and pray, and seek My face and turn from their wicked ways, then I will hear from heaven, will forgive their sin, and will heal their land."

The first action is humiliation and prayer. Prayer cannot be over-emphasized in this process. Prayer movements today in our nation, 24/7 houses of prayer, and prayer marches are all essential to unite the church in intercession for the nation. Churches must start prayer meetings that focus on the nation instead of themselves. Churches must develop unity with other Christians and churches in prayer events. Research and prayer will uncover local and regional demonic strongholds. After discovery, Christians can then resist demonic activity with prophetic proclamation. A united church can then pray and prophetically proclaim these seven characteristics to come alive in the hearts of the all the people and leaders of society.

However, if one believes this alone will be enough, it is a serious deception. Prayer, evangelism and revival alone have never completely changed any nation in over 2000 years of church history.

Prayers must be accompanied with a strategy of raising up leaders for the nation. A nation's decline never occurs because various secular organizations have overcome Biblical ideas. The church abdicates its responsibility to lead and leaves a void or vacuum in the public realm, surrendering by default. Even if there are enough Christian leaders in society today with a strong Biblical worldview, there must also be a unified strategy, teamwork that is only concerned with God receiving the glory, and long-term plans and goals will bring transformation. It is not massive numbers, it is a focused few.

Churches must emphasize the importance of teaching the Bible for all areas of life that develop, support, and send out those who understand the importance of a missional approach to cultural change. Together, pastors and business leaders must strategize to create new initiatives and ongoing services for advanced training of professionals in their spheres of influence. This includes returning seminaries to a clear understanding of pastoral leadership and 5-fold ministry that teaches about nations.

Finally, churches must do more than just teach and train. They must send out these leaders into their areas of influence. Pastors and business leaders must form or join organizations that are doing strategic planning, credentialing, and placement of upcoming leaders in influential positions for the transformation of nations in all seven areas.

"Speaking the Nation's New Tongues"

There are three fundamental action strategies to help Christians deal with community ignorance and error and help the community to "Speak with new tongues":

- Parents and teachers providing home or church-based education of children
- Restoring Universities to Biblical Worldview to include the 7 mountain concept or start new ones
- Get Arts and Media to include biblical worldview of culture and national affairs (not just salvation)

God caused the nations to "speak with new tongues" at Babel in order to stop the centralization of power and enslavement of people under Nimrod. Jesus likewise told his followers to disciple the nations. If they did their job well He expected them to see the nations "speak with new tongues." Their mission was battle for the soul and mind of the people in their cities and countries by becoming influential voices in the schools and media.

Christians must win the ear of culture by being involved in education and communication at the highest level of professional excellence. When Christians are in positions at Harvard or Hollywood, they gain the ear of the public with a "tongue" that unites people. Speaking God's language of liberty rooted in the Bible empowers good people to liberate their nation while rejecting immoral and statist institutions and men whose worldview and morals lead to spiritual and cultural bondage.

Training parents, teachers, professors, artists and journalists to "speak with a new tongue" will transform a nation. First, churches must emphasize the parent's role in education and develop plans to train and supplement those who wish to home school. The church must be persistent in this truth because the brainwashing that only the state can successfully educate is strong. The idea that "it won't work" will be a normal reaction but once new models begin to bear fruit, naysayers will be silenced. Parents and grandparents must begin to strategize and find a way to work together, creating the income needed and still teach their children at home. If impossible, cooperate with other families and churches. Christians must form or join cooperative organizations that train, equip, and connect home-schooling parents, not just in one church but in the community at large.

To transform teachers and universities, churches must emphasize the missionary role not of the children but of teachers and professors in government schools while developing plans to train, support, and send out those who are called and equipped to be salt and light in the universities. Pastors and business leaders must work together to create new Christian elementary schools that can serve the non-Christian community, especially the poor who cannot afford to go to private schools. Parents, working with pastors and business leaders, must begin to find ways to help establish cooperative organizations to supplement parents in their teaching role at home, much like the Levites did in Israel.

Pastors, professors, and business leaders must work together to create new Christian colleges and universities that become the best institutions of higher learning in the country. Also believers should form or join organizations that train, equip, and support good teachers and professors, especially those who train in a true biblical worldview and the principle approach teaching method. Pastors should also work to get bible schools and seminaries to include a theology for all of life (civil government, etc), not just about church.

In order to transform artists and journalists, churches must emphasize the missionary role of artists and journalists while developing plans to train, support, and send out. Pastors and business leaders must work together to create new film studios, television networks, and newspapers that can serve the non-Christian community. In addition, churches need to form or join organizations that train, equip, and support good artists and journalists, especially those that will train them to communicate in a true biblical worldview.

"Taking Up the Nation's Serpents"

In conclusion, there are three fundamental action strategies to help Christians
deal with injustice and tyranny and help the community to "Take Up Serpents":

- Limiting government to protection and punishing corruption in taxes, banking, spending and labor
- Voting for good government
- Opposing tyranny and injustice with protest, flight and defensive force

God liberated the nations in the past through efforts of His people to serve in politics. Jesus told his followers to disciple the nations and that he expected them to also "take up serpents." In other words, like Moses, they would have to confront the "pharaohs" of their nations. Is not politics where we find most of the snakes? Ignore it and nation cannot never be completely changed.

The Great Commission of Jesus then means we must also become effective in the battle against corruption and injustice in society.

First, the basic limited purpose of government as defined in the Bible must be recovered and emphasized. Then, when possible, this limited purpose must be enshrined in each nation with a constitution that keeps that purpose in place over many generations.

Second, Christians must overcome the evil in politics by modeling godly practices in voting, advising government, submitting to good law. Their government practices must be at the highest level of professional excellence. When Christians are in positions at the top of governments, then they can begin to replace the pagan approach that looks to the state to solve most problems and takes away more and more of the liberty and property of the people.

Finally, it must be acknowledged that in a fallen sinful world, more often government power is going to be abused or at the least, misguided in attempts to solve problems the way God never intended for the state to do – leading to more problems. Therefore, the third way that godly people must act to overcome corruption and tyranny is to speak up and protest peacefully against injustice. When government itself becomes corrupt, then peaceful protest is often unable to bring change. Then the option of emigration becomes necessary. Finally, if that option seems impossible, then the last option is to use force to defend oneself or others being oppressed. But even then it is only allowed if believers can persuade a lower government official to deputize citizens to resist and fight against the higher officials that are perverting the law.

Christians have applied these practices over the last 2000 years and have thus changed the history of the world.

"Drinking the nation's deadly things"

There are three fundamental action strategies to help Christians deal with corruption and poverty and helping the community to "Drink deadly things and not be harmed":
- Working, Doing business and trade
- Banking
- Giving

God liberated the nations in the past through efforts of His people to serve in business. Jesus told his followers to disciple the nations and that he expected them to also "drink anything deadly." In other words they would have to confront the "deadly things" of their nations. Is not business and finance where we find most of the corrupting influence? Ignore it and nation cannot never be completely changed.

The Great Commission of Jesus then means we must also become effective in the battle against corruption and poverty in society.

Christians must overcome the evil in business by modeling godly patterns in work, business and in trade.

Diligence and excellence in the workplace comes first. Their business practices must be at the highest level of professional excellence. When Christians are in positions at the top of corporations, then they can begin to replace the pagan approach.

Being good in business, leads to the growth of our property and resources that then requires of a stewardship responsibility. We must enter the marketplace and learn to trade in order to both grow our own wealth but also to gain respect and influence the community for good.

Besides simply being excellent in our business, the Bible tells us to save and invest our resources together in a cooperative way by creating banks and financial institutions that we lead in a manner that is different from the world. Honest money and banking is important, but with the added view to making those pooled resources available for other institutions and individual initiatives that really are healthy for society.

Finally, the biblical best practice that transcends all others in community is a commitment to compassionate giving of finances for the needy. Christians must win the hearts of the popular culture by being involved in practical acts of compassion for their physical, emotional, and financial needs. Christian health care must be at the highest level of professional excellence.

Instead of looking to the state to solve most problems, which ends up just taking away more and more of the liberty and property of the people, Christians working cooperatively can begin to replace failed government handouts with real compassion. There is no personal righteousness in the coercive state taking taxes from everyone for the poor. The poor never feel real love and compassion when it receives money from government and they begin to feel entitled to it and lose the incentive to change. Human beings alone caring for their neighbors, is the key to meeting needs and helping get people back on a path of lasting independence and dignity.

To raise up the church that defeats poverty, the church must train individuals, churches and business people to work together. First churches must emphasize the personal responsibility of each person to care for the poor. Then churches can also help those with a mission to serve the poor to work together in a coordinated fashion by using coordinated funds and talents. Pastors and business leaders must strategize to find a way to work together to create new community funds and to manage them effectively. If not yet legal, then churches should begin to talk to their political leaders to establish the right to have private services for the poor and to manage funds for the purpose without interference from the state. Finally, believers should form or join organizations that train, equip and support those who are caring for the poor and needy.

Christianity has changed the world with its work ethic and compassionate giving.

"Laying Hands on the Nation's Sicknesses"

There are three fundamental action strategies to help Christians deal with disease and divisions and helping the community to "Lay Hands on the Sick":

- Doctors and nurses teaching health and applying Medicine consistent with biblical worldview
- Families, Businesses & churches providing help for the elderly and emergency relief for disaster victims
- Churches touching and reconciling racial, tribal, religious, economic and age divisions

God healed the nations in the past through efforts of His people to serve in reconciliation, health care, and emergency aid for victims of disasters. Jesus told his followers to disciple the nations and that he expected them to also "lay hands on the sick" individuals and nations. Their mission was to become effective in the battle for rescuing the wounded, hurting and downtrodden in society.

When Christians are in positions at the top private hospitals and charitable agencies, they can begin to replace the pagan approach. We need to get families, doctors, relief workers, and business leaders trained to "heal the nation."

To train and mobilize doctors and health care workers to "heal the nation's sicknesses," churches must emphasize the missionary role of those in the health care field and develop plans to train, support, and send out those who desire to do. Christians should also form or join organizations that train and support health care professionals but also develop new medical schools to train in a non-pagan medical ethic.

Emergency organizations must be raised up or supported with better moral leadership if they already exist. Pastors and business leaders must begin to strategize to find a way to work together to create new clinics and services for those who cannot afford it. The same is true for emergency aid organizations. If not yet legal, then churches should begin to talk to their political leaders about establishing the right to have private medical services and medical schools, and emergency relief organizations that are uncontrolled by the state and its pagan ethics.

Churches must emphasize the importance of efforts at reconciliation and develop plans to train, support, and send out those who desire to do. Pastors and business leaders must begin to strategize to find a way to work together to create new initiatives and ongoing services to reach out to those who are wounded and alienated, forming or joining organizations that are already doing reconciliation.

Chapter 14

A Practical Agenda for National Transformation

<u>Five Steps to Transform Society</u>

In the next few paragraphs we will summarize the way Christians did it in the past when nations were significantly transformed. Often they were never but a small percentage of the population but when they did these things, they succeeded to turn their nations. These patterns have been used by pagans as well with success.

A modern example is the homosexual community. Although under 2% of the population in the United States, they applied this strategy and in under 50 years have captured the power bases of culture, especially in schools and media, and are now changing opinion of the general public to accept their lifestyle because of speaking their perverse "tongue" unceasingly through these institutions. In a similar way, the secular pagan movements in America deliberately developed a plan in 2002 that was coordinated by the "Thunder Road Group" that basically is what Christians used to do, but now is being used against them effectively.

There is nothing wrong for other groups to do what Christians should be doing, so it is not worth focusing on them as if they are a conspiracy. Rather, we simply must get back to doing these things that really will move God's kingdom forward effectively. If we do, other groups who promote philosophies and goals contrary to that, will lose.

There are seven strategic resources that we must create or multiply and connect:
- *new organizations working on each of the 7 cultural areas*

- *organizations to do opposition research*
- *think tanks to provide research for strategy and winning arguments*
- *social technology*
- *media operations*
- *mobilization organizations for voting, protesting, and other best-practices*
- *coordinated giving and funding organizations*

The church today may be growing in numbers and having "mega-church" assemblies but is still losing the culture. This is true even though they are much larger in numbers than homosexuals or any other pagan group. It must recognize its failure and stop "business as usual" and return to a truly biblical model that the historic church applied to disciple nations. We are ineffective today because there is no unified strategy.

Of course, it makes sense that denominations and churches separately have legitimate purposes and honest differences of belief that may not allow them to build churches together, but that should not prevent us to unite for the good of our communities. We can keep our liturgical preferences but we can be united in our common biblical worldview and on our transformational great commission mission.

Throughout this book we have identified best practices that Christians did in united fashion in many different cultures over the past two millennia and were historically powerful in 7 areas: politics, business, education, medicine, media, church and family. In each of these areas, it was done on the local level first. We must not be frozen in a mistaken notion that someone has to start this nationally before we can do anything. No the local level is real power to shape history. Only when it is happening locally is it possible to connect regionally and nationally in a meaningful way.

Most organizations tend to start top down. This is a mistake. They often want to create one organization identified with one person. This is a mistake. As soon as the enemy is able to demonize and stigmatize that group, the movement stops being effective. No. We must build locally and build diverse organizations. If one group is targeted and stereotyped negatively by the enemy, then let it die and work through a new group. That's the way to win. But we have to have a mindset that God's kingdom goes on even though organizations fade. And to do this strategy that means we don't care what humans get the credit on earth. Local organizations can be coordinated behind the scenes with a unified strategy and it cannot be stopped.

We must begin to work long-term, strategic and united in the following five steps.

5 steps that will transform society if done in each community:

1. Provide *general education* in the Discipling Nations Transformation vision

- In each local community we need more of the Christian community to learn about Christ's truly great commission to disciple nations so that many more believers may become mobilized beyond merely winning souls for heaven and building churches. Good organizations already may exist that can help in this general educational step and especially pastors should be able to do this.

2. Identify and provide *advanced training* for leaders in all 5 signs and 7 cultural institutions.

- In each local community we need those who get awakened to the discipling nations vision to find somewhere to receive more training. It's not enough to simply be motivated but then go out with an unrenewed mind. We have to have in-depth teaching available on the local level (ideally in every local church to some degree) on the biblical best practices and worldview principles for each of the 7 spheres of influence. Again, good organizations already exist that can help with this advanced training step. Most pastors may not feel adequate to do it, but can employ these other teaching ministries to help supplement their church's basic discipleship.

3. Connect trained leaders in these professional fields into *networked teams*

- In the first two steps there is some degree of activity that exists but now we begin to see with this step where Christians are most in need of change. In each local community there are usually a few trained believers working in the 7 cultural areas of influence, but they are largely limited in their impact precisely because they are acting independently of each other. They work alone and isolated instead of as a team. So now in each local community we need to identify who these trained individuals are and begin to connect them to each other in networks and teams that can pull in the same direction. The ATC especially is helping at this stage in various cities across the nation. There are sometimes some professional networks and some Christian groups bringing fellowship for businessmen or teachers or health care workers, etc. No group has to yield to another or dissolve. Each are important. But these need to be brought into awareness of each other and then be willing to embrace the idea of strategic planning and action. No organization has to lose its purpose and identity in this process. Rather, the networking step helps every organization to be more well known and more effective, not less.

4. **Execute long-term *strategic action plans for each of these professional fields.***

- Another key but least common step is the creation of long-term strategic plans for each of the 7 cultural teams and then the integration of those plans into a comprehensive city-wide plan that is comprehensive of all the mountains or gates of influence. Even in the rare occurrence today of a Christian city-wide transformation council, it is almost overwhelmingly focused on prayer events, fellowship, and if there are actions that are planned, it is usually short-term and defensive in nature to stop evil things happening. Real transformation in nations over the past 2000 years has only come when there has been an intentional plan to get leaders into the highest and many of the critical positions of the influential institutions of society.

Today and in history, sometimes a Christian has gotten elected to high office or become a major leader in media or medicine, for example, but because not enough of other believers are also in lower positions or equal positions in parallel institutions, the rare leader is largely ineffective due to so many pagan leaders pushing back against anything they want to do. The rare Christian leader at a high position is also eventually discouraged or compromised in some way by the constant pressure of the opposition and temptation against him. We often also try to convert people at the top or claim them as allies when in reality more often than not they are using the church and they have no in-depth understanding of how to bring transformation in the Biblical way. So the church gets a bad reputation or discouraged.

Success is absolutely dependent on a long-term strategy to raise up an entire movement of biblically trained leaders in the 7 cultural areas that slowly get placed into key positions through the recommendations and advocacy of existing Christian leaders. Over time these earn experience, as well as credentials from institutions that the world respects, not just the church, and prove themselves worthy of higher positions. This process takes time but within about 20 to 30 years a young leader can become a top political leader, or top banker or Hollywood producer, or Hospital administrator, or University President, Dean or professor, or television network owner or news anchor, or top CEO or owner of a Fortune 500 company, etc, etc. You get the idea. But that's when REAL transformation can begin to happen.

For that to be possible the city-wide strategic councils must develop plans to be at the top of those institutions in 50 years, and then they must start counting backward to create real benchmarks, goals, and plan of work that leads back to the coming year ahead. Then instead of just activity that is reacting to what pagans are doing, we have our own plan and our activity the coming year, and then 5 years down the road, etc, has real meaning and significance.

This of course means we must have leaders who are willing to work hard even though they may not see all that much change in their own lifetime, but will be satisfied that their children or grandchildren will enjoy its fruit. As the Pilgrims said, they knew they were but as "stepping stones unto others for so great a work." Church leaders have to be willing to let their best people give time to these community institutions and not demand them to keep all their focus on church activities. Church leaders must also accept the reality that they must send their best people away to places like Wall Street or Hollywood or Harvard or Washington so that they can get credibility and be raised up to change the power bases of the culture. Many times they may return to local community but the pastor must affirm those young leaders with this vision and send them out.

The ATC is strongly casting this vision and coaching local leadership teams to begin to think long-term like this. As more and more believers catch the vision and are brought into the local strategic plan, they will bring new perspectives and talents and resources and vision that will constantly cause the local plan to be tweaked and improved. This should always be welcome as long as it meets the worldview principles and biblical best practices criteria.

5. **Develop *funding* for permanent *institutions* in these *professional fields***

- The final step must not be overlooked. Often vision dies when the original visionaries die or are not able to contribute anymore for some reason. Even if the original strategic leadership remain involved, there is rarely big transformation without a concurrent plan for sustainable funding of the strategic plan. A good plan will not rely solely on donations but will develop a business model for making it financially-self-sustaining. This is why a local city-wide team must incorporate all of the 7 mountain team plans into a master plan and then leaders from every sector of the community can see where the needs are and entrepreneurs can find what they would like to do help fulfill it with an existing or new business. New hospitals or movie studios or universities or political parties will emerge qualitatively different from the world and will truly make a difference. It is amazing how much money is made available from the very Christian businessmen who no longer feel that excited about simply another church facility that sits largely empty most of the week and irrelevant to the real institutions that change the world.

Concluding Thoughts:

Certainly as local plans and teams develop there will come opportunity to work in coordination with other cities in their region and state, and even nationwide. This leads to constant enrichment and development of state and national strategy that may have truly historical impact. In fact, when this has emerged this way in the past, it ALWAYS has led to significant national reformation and transformation.

Leaders must articulate this vision and for local strategic planning groups in each community and set long-term goals. What is the ideal they hope to achieve in 50 years? Then they have to work backwards to goals for next year. And then stick with it. Don't quit. Share it with the next generation and incorporate young leaders into the steering committee so that it does not die with the original organizers of the strategic plan. It must be multi-generational and long-term in order to work.

Visionaries all over the world are arising in recent years with this dream. Most have yet to hear of them. The news is dominated by stories that seem to indicate the world is getting worse, but a powerful new undercurrent is already flowing. The fruit of their work will surely come but perhaps in the next generation. Don't be impatient and short in your vision. And it doesn't matter what your eschatology is. Even if one thinks Jesus is going to return very soon, He has never changed His commission to us. Occupy until He returns (Luke 19:13)! Go and disciple the nations!

APPENDIX

A Self-Assessment for Leaders

Revival and church growth alone has never fully transformed a nation in two millennia of church history. But when church leaders have strategically focused on raising up leaders for society, then nations have changed. There are at least Seven Mountains ("high places") of cultural influence. These seven areas are the battlefields where a society or culture will be won or lost for the Kingdom of God.

Jesus never said to go and win souls or plant churches, but in Matthew 28:20 he did say to preach to all creatures and "make disciples of all nations" by the method of "teaching them to observe all things whatsoever I have commanded you." In the parallel passage in Mark 16 Jesus added "signs" that would follow this mission. In other words, there was a way to measure progress of discipling nations. A model nation is one where the Biblical principles are being taught in all seven areas and where networks of support and strategic coordination are established for these.

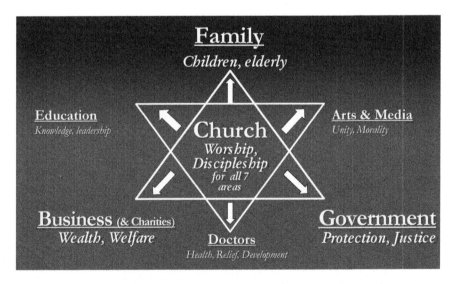

Church is one of the seven key influential spheres of a nation, but its mission is especially to disciple leaders for the other six areas.

Therefore, church leadership needs to intentionally have a plan for the other six areas. Therefore, a checklist is provided on the next page to help a church to assess its progress and develop a plan. It is a suggested list of "kingdom practices" rooted in the Bible that are effective in transforming culture. Use it to stimulate your thinking and add your own ideas.

If you would like more indepth explanation of each of the items below with Scriptural support, please contact the Global Transformation Network president Dr. Mark Beliles with your questions at www.nationaltransformation.com or by email at nationaltransformation@gmail.com

Measuring Discipleship of Seven "Mountains" of Culture

Is your church intentionally providing teaching and mentoring in the following areas? Does it provide a structure for sustainable action? Check off each item & put a date to act. Use back to list resources needed.

1. **Practices in Marriage & Family**   Yes   No   Date
   Monogamous heterosexual marriage
   Bear multiple children
   Provide godly education
   Provide courtship oversight
   Double portion of savings
   Repaying parents with in-home retirement care
   Restricted divorce

2. **Practices in Business & Work**   Yes   No   Date
   Labor six days; Rest one day
   Money management: Trade & invest to multiply wealth
   Tithing
   Setting aside for poor
   Gleaning opportunity in your business
   Community strategic fund

3. **Practices in Medicine & Relief**   Yes   No   Date
   Provide coordinated savings fund
   Provide coop health care and relief services for members
   Medicine and relief training
   Medicine and relief support and mentoring/testimonies
   Provide medicine and relief dept/administrator/equipment
   Support missionary health care/relief ministries to secular institutions
   Coordinate with others to start & help new hospitals, relief agencies

4. **Practices in Schools & Colleges**   Yes   No   Date
   Regular Worldview seminars for members
   Parental education training
   Parental education support and mentoring/testimonies
   Provide coop for home-school parents and schools
   Provide a school/administrator/facilities
   Support missionary teachers & ministries to secular schools & colleges
   Coordinate with others to start & help new universities

5. **Practices in Arts & Media**   Yes   No   Date
   Provide social media evaluation, reviews, critical seminars
   Provide accountability resources/technology for members
   Arts and Media and journalism training
   Arts and Media and journalism support and mentoring, testimonies
   Provide arts and media and journalism dept, administrator, equipment
   Support missionary artists, and ministries to secular institutions
   Coordinate with others to start/help papers, tv-stations, film studios,etc

6. **Practices in Citizenship & Justice**   Yes   No   Date
   Submit to just law and governors
   Give taxes and info and aid to good governors
   Resist/protest injustice (even governors)
   Study law and candidate information
   Organize voter education (endorse candidates)
   Vote for character and worldview
   Be armed and use in self-defense if necessary

The Global Transformation Network

In the 2000 years of church history many examples show where Christians had a huge impact in transforming their nations. Unfortunately, much of that has stopped happening in modern times due to a narrowing of their mission to simply winning souls and growing churches. We must return to a truly biblical model that the historic church applied to disciple nations in 7 areas: politics, business, education, medicine, media, church and family. This vision is long-term, strategic and proven to succeed.

5 steps that our Transformation Network does in each nation:
1. Provide *general education* in 5 signs Transformation vision
2. Identify and provide *advanced training* for 5 signs leaders
3. Connect trained 5 signs leaders into *networked teams*
4. Execute long-term *strategic 5 signs action plans*
5. Develop *funding* for permanent 5 signs *institutions*

In the next decade our vision is to have a strategic network working in every major city and nation around the globe. These networks will have annual regional and national transformation summits to gather the leaders of each local network for encouragement and sharing of expertise. A national team will provide ongoing coaching and assistance to the leaders in different cities and will develop and provide a Transformation Toolbox with books, dvds, podcasts, and internet online courses. These national leaders will also be able to connect with others from different nations in their region of the world who are doing similar things and facing similar problems.

Contact the Global team to find out how to join or start a network in your area
Contact us and tell us if you have interest or expertise in one or more of the 7 areas. If you have leadership gifts, we are looking for people to help create and facilitate local transformation teams. Go to our webpage at www.NationalTransformation.com or via email at NationalTransformation@gmail.com   or USA website:
www.AmericaTransformationCompany.com

Recommended Resources

This book is an introduction. If you want more in-depth teaching on the 7 spheres of influence and how to really get practical in transformation of a nation then get the five part teaching series called...

The Strategic Discipleship of Culture:

> **Cast Out a Nation's Demons**
> **Speak a Nation's New Tongues**
> **Take up a Nation's Serpents**
> **Drink a Nation's Deadly Things**
> **Lay Hands on a Nation's Sicknesses**

DVDs of this course are also available as well as online courses that are fully accredited.

To order these and many other books, dvds and online resources go to www.AmericaTransformationCompany.com or www.NationalTransformation.com
Or (Espanol: www.TransformacionGlobal.com)

Also see www.AmericaPublications.com

Mark Beliles Biographical Information

Dr. Mark A. Beliles is president of the Global Transformation Network and it's USA branch called the America Transformation Company. Beliles is a popular speaker and cultural leadership coach who has traveled to over 50 countries and addressed parliaments and high-level leaders of nations on the topic of faith and freedom. South African members of parliament have given to Beliles official tokens of recognition for his contribution to their successful transition away from apartheid. Beliles also serves as the North American facilitator in the global Transform World 2020 movement and one of the leaders of the Reconciled Church, the 4-14 Window, and other movements.

He founded an educational ministry called the Providence Foundation in 1983 and its Biblical Worldview University, and co-authored other books for popular audiences such as *America's Providential History* and *Contending for the Constitution: Recalling the Christian Influence on the Writing of the Constitution and the Biblical Basis of American Law and Liberty*, and *Liberating the Nations* and several other books just for international audiences.

Beliles, an ordained minister since 1977, has served as pastor of various non-denominational churches for over 35 years and was the founder of Grace Covenant Church in Charlottesville, Virginia. He has provided apostolic oversight to dozens of churches in the U.S. and abroad and today serves on the Apostolic Council of the International Communion of Evangelical Churches (presiding Bishop Harry Jackson). Beliles earned his Ph.D. from Whitefield Theological Seminary.

He has organized, with sponsorship of the Virginia Foundation for the Humanities, several scholarly symposiums held at the University of Virginia on Jefferson and religion that each featured dozens of nationally-known Jefferson scholars and church and state historians. He has served for many years as Chairman of the Charlottesville Historic Resources Committee and co-chairman of the city's 250th Anniversary observed in 2012. Beliles' most recent scholarly books on Thomas Jefferson are *Doubting Thomas?-The Religious Life and Legacy of Thomas Jefferson* and *The Selected Religious Letters and Papers of Thomas Jefferson.* (at www.AmericaPublications.com)

He and his wife Nancy homeschooled their three children and now are blessed with eight grandchildren.

Made in the
USA
Middletown, DE